BLACK ELK SPEAKS

Based on the book

by

JOHN G. NEIHARDT

Adapted for the stage

by

CHRISTOPHER SERGEL

Dramatic Publishing
Woodstock, Illinois • London, England • Melbourne, Australia

INTRODUCTION

*"O six Powers of the World hear me in my sorrow
for I may never call again...
O make my people live."*

Black Elk, standing on the highest peak in the Black Hills, spoke these words that give purpose to our play.

The dramatic riches of the source materials on which this play is based derive from Black Elk's direct involvement in many pivotal events of Indian history, from his vision, and from his extraordinary eloquence.

Black Elk lived the experience of the Native American people from a time just before white people entered his part of the world through the end of Indian independence in the massacre at Wounded Knee. His participation was immediate and personal. As a child, he saw his father return wounded from the Fetterman Battle and as the family fled with the father carried on a pony drag, so also began a lifetime of temporary habitation and flight for the Prairie Sioux. In the midst of this, when Black Elk was nine years old and quite ill, he had a vision that related to the meaning of life as it could be for all men; a vision which later became central to much of the spiritual life of all Native Americans.

Against the unusual beauty of his religious experience and that of a vital young man who would be among the last to know traditional life, there is the relentless pressure of the bluecoat soldiers, settlers and gold-seekers astride Manifest Destiny. Black Elk was swimming in the Little Big Horn when he saw the approach of Reno's detachment, riding in advance of Custer's main force, and though only thirteen, he fought in that battle. He is one of the few authentic sources of the history of the great Indian warrior and spiritual leader

Crazy Horse. He knew Crazy Horse, his second cousin, intimately and was present at Fort Robinson when Crazy Horse was killed. He was involved in the Ghost Dance religion with its hope for an Indian messiah, the return of the buffalo, and the resurrection of those who had been killed. Finally, Black Elk was present and badly wounded at the massacre at Wounded Knee.

Much later in life, Black Elk spoke of all these things to his friend, the poet and historian John G. Neihardt, a man who was uniquely able to capture this experience and this eloquence.

John G. Neihardt, widely recognized as one of our great poets, travelled to the Pine Ridge Reservation to spend time with the elderly Black Elk and together they explored this history and the spiritual world of Native America. From this came the acclaimed classic BLACK ELK SPEAKS.

And from that came this play.

Retracing Neihardt's steps, the playwright also spent time at Pine Ridge where he met with descendants of Black Elk. The playwright received help and insights from Black Elk's daughter Lucy who had been present at the meetings between her father and John Neihardt. Also present at those meetings was Neihardt's daughter Hilda, who became another important source for the play. Camping together beside Wounded Knee we explored—as earlier it had been explored by John Neihardt—this experience and this eloquence.

Wounded Knee today is as described by Black Elk, but instead of the guns on the high ground there's a weed-covered mass grave with a small stone memorial beside it which reads, in part, "Here died many women and children who knew no wrong."

Black Elk is their voice as he's a voice for all Indian people. When you do this play, then you become that voice.

This new version of *BLACK ELK SPEAKS* was produced by the Denver Center Theatre company where it opened on September 24, 1993.

Directed by .... Donovan Marley
Set Design .... Bill Curley
Costume Design .... Andrew V. Yelusich
Light Design .... Don Darnutzer
Sound Design .... David R. White
Assistant Director .... Anthony Powell
Choreography .... Jane Lind
Musical Direction and Composition .... Dennis Yerry

The cast included:

Ned Romero .... Black Elk
Kennetch Charlette .... Hoksila

The Other Relatives:
John Belindo ..... Cherokee Chief, Pilgrim, Betting Soldier,
                Galbraith, Cheyenne Chief, Sherman, Crook
Jack Burning .. The Elder, Betting Navajo, Santee War Party,
                Black Kettle, Arapaho Chief
Lorne Cardinal ..... Taino Chief, Young Navajo, Shakopee,
                Wynkoop, Red Cloud, Flag Soldier, Crook's Aide
Bernard Cottonwood .... Musician
Gregory Norman Cruz .. Columbus, Manuelito, Spirit Guide,
                Chivington, Soldier Aide, Torch Dancer, Sergeant
Luke Dubray .. Naragansett Chief, Soldier, Santee War Party,
                Fancy Dancer
Stephen C. Dubray .... Musician
Peter Kelly Gaudreault .. Colonial Soldier, Corporal, Norton,
                Medicine Bottle, Cramer, Crazy Horse, Custer

Darrel Zephier Ironwing .... Musician

Jane Lind .... Lucy, Yellow Woman, Eagle Dancer

Kenneth Little Hawk .... Musician, Cheyenne Chief
Crazy Horse's Father

Hawk Loon . . Seminole Chief, Priest, Sibley, Cheyenne Chief,
Carrington, Soldier

Dara Marin . . . Navajo Girl, Bosque Refugee, Cheyenne Girl,
Lakota Child

Kenneth Martines . . . Jackson, General Carleton, Little Crow,
William Bent, Commissioner Taylor, Finerty

David Medina . . . . Taino Man, Lt. Ortiz, Carleton's Aide,
Wowinapa, Flag Soldier

Jill Scott Momaday .... Taino Woman, Navajo,
Cheyenne Woman, Soldier, Magpie, Fancy Dancer

Gracie Red Shirt-Tyon . . . Navajo Woman, Cheyenne Woman,
.... Soldier, Lakota Woman, Fancy Dancer

Maria Antoinette Rogers ..... Grandmother, Navajo Woman,
Santee Woman, Soldier, Crazy Horse's Mother,
Queen Victoria

Tachara Maraya Salazar .... Taino Girl, Navajo Girl,
Bosque Refugee, Cheyenne, Lakota Child

Larry Swalley ...... Pequot Chief, Navajo, Santee War Party,
Soldier, Fancy Dancer

Stephan Ray Swimmer .... Mohawk Chief, Clown Spirit,
Santee War Party, Hoop Dancer, Soldier, Fancy Dancer

Kateri Walker .... Taino Woman, Navajo Woman,
Crossover Spirit, Soldier, Lakota Woman, Fancy Dancer

Dennis Yerry .... Musician

The Denver Center Theatre Company re-mounted its production, opened it on September 23, 1994, then co-produced the play with the Mark Taper Forum in Los Angeles where it opened January 3, 1995.

This cast included:

Ned Romero . . . . Black Elk
David Medina . . . . Hoksila
John Belindo . . . . Crook and ensemble
Stuart Bird . . . . Shakopee and ensemble
Seth Bissonette . . . . Musician and ensemble
Jack Burning . . . . Black Kettle and ensemble
Bernard Cottonwood . . . . Musician and ensemble
Luke Dubray . . . . Dancer and ensemble
James Fall . . . . Wowinapa and ensemble
Peter Kelly Gaudreault . . . Crazy Horse, Custer and ensemble
Dane Lebeau . . . . Musician and ensemble
Jane Lind . . . . Yellow Woman and ensemble
Kenneth Little Hawk . Musician, Crazy Horse's Father, ensemble
Kenneth Martines . . . . Little Crow and ensemble
Miguel Najera . . . . Manuelito and ensemble
Gracie Red Shirt-Tyon . . . . Dancer and ensemble
Andrew Roa . . . . Red Cloud and ensemble
Maria Antoinette Rogers . . . . . . Queen Victoria and ensemble
Tachara Maraya Salazar . . . . Ensemble
Adan Sanchez . . . . Columbus and ensemble
Larry Swalley . . . . Medicine Bottle and ensemble
Stephan Ray Swimmer . . . . Hoop Dancer and ensemble
Kateri Walker . . . . Crossover Spirit and ensemble
Dennis Yerry . . . . Musician and ensemble

with special thanks to
THE BLACK ELK FAMILY
and
DONOVAN MARLEY

ACT ONE

SCENE 1A
On and near Harney Peak, South Dakota
October 1931

(There is no curtain. The majority of the stage floor is en-
closed in a circle that is defined by a huge red hoop. The
hoop is made of twelve curved wooden sticks decorated
with leather thongs. Behind the hoop are several rock
ledges, including one high peak. The ledges and a series of
platforms made from lodge poles create a ridge from one
side of the stage to the other; behind the ridge is a vast
sky. From half-hour to curtain time, the sound of wind
singing through the pine trees of the Black Hills is heard.
This sound is occasionally punctuated by bird songs and
animal calls. In the distance, occasional rumbles of thun-
der can be heard. As curtain time grows near, the sounds
intensify and the wind rises.

At curtain time all lights go out. The stage is dark. A wind
is blowing. It is just before dawn. There is a clap of thun-
der; a stab of lightning silhouettes a naked FIGURE at the
top of the highest peak. The FIGURE tosses a handful of
sage onto a hidden fire. As the fire flares up, the FIGURE
stands, and we see that it is an old man. His long white
hair falls around his shoulders; his face has the classic
features of a Lakota elder in his late sixties. THE OLD
MAN wears only a leather breechclout and moccasins;
with the exception of his hands and face, his body is cov-

9

ered in red paint. With smoke from the fire rising around his face, he offers the mouthpiece of his Chanupa [the sacred pipe of the Lakota people] to the four directions, calling "hey-ah-hey" to each of them.)

THE OLD MAN. Great Spirit, my grandfathers, lean close to the earth to hear the voice I send. You have been always. You are older than all need, older than pain, older than prayer. My grandfathers, all over the earth the faces of living things are alike. Look upon your children, with children in their arms, that they may face the winds and walk the good red road to the day of quiet. Teach us to walk the soft earth, a relative to all that is. My grandfathers, you said to me that in difficulty I should send a voice. Grandfathers, night after night I send a voice...*(He is interrupted by a rumble of thunder. Rising above the thunder is a VOICE calling to THE OLD MAN in Lakota.)* The only reply, "It is time. You must hurry." *(Another rumble of thunder in which the VOICE calls again. Urgently.)* You gave me a mission, but I do not know how to fulfill it. The tree does not live, the hoop is broken...*(Another rumble of thunder with the VOICE is heard. THE OLD MAN begins to pray feverishly in Lakota.)*

Tunkasila Huhapi Waciwakia...

(His voice trails off as a BOY of about seventeen enters with a wooden bowl filled with water. The BOY is dressed in clothes that an aspiring college freshman from the midwest might have worn in 1931, including a tie and a coat. His black hair is so tightly tied that it appears to be short. His name, HOKSILA, means both "boy" and "the boy in each of us" in his native Lakota language. HOKSILA calls up to the peak.)

HOKSILA. Grandfather!

(From the depths of his trance, THE OLD MAN cannot hear him. We now discover that two male RELATIVES of THE OLD MAN have been sitting patiently at the base of the levels UC; they are dressed in worn wasichu [white man] clothing common on Indian reservations in 1931. The RELATIVES rise to confront HOKSILA.)

THE ELDER. Hoksila, he is praying.

HOKSILA. For four days he's eaten nothing. You want him to get sick? *(The ELDER eyes him firmly.)* At least take him this water. *(HOKSILA explodes.)* I won't let my grandfather die for some crazy Indian superstition.

(THE OLD MAN hears the explosion and leaves his trance to stare at HOKSILA. The THREE below are unaware of THE OLD MAN. A WOMAN of about forty enters. She is dressed in colorless, shapeless reservation wear. She carries a bundle of clothes; her name is LUCY.)

LUCY. Hoksila! Are you making trouble?

HOKSILA. Why does your father come here?

LUCY. To pray, and to wait.

HOKSILA. For what?

LUCY. Ask him.

HOKSILA. That's all our old men do, sift reservation dust through their hands, and wait! Nothing ever happens here! *(HOKSILA falls silent when he senses that THE OLD MAN is looking down at him.)*

LUCY. Ask him. *(HOKSILA does not respond. She calls up to the peak.)* For what do you wait, my father?

THE OLD MAN. For what does any old Indian wait? He waits for yesterday. But all that comes again is the memory. I will come down. *(As he turns, his weakened body gives way; he sways precariously and must steady himself. HOKSILA and the TWO MEN leap forward to climb the peak and assist him. LUCY stops HOKSILA.)*

LUCY. Not you. It must be the ones who took him there. *(THE OLD MAN exits.)*

HOKSILA. Do you really believe it makes a difference who brings him down? Mother? *(Without speaking she spreads a blanket on the ground and begins to lay out a moist towel, a man's shirt and a well-worn black sack suit.)* It's 1931! Yesterday is gone. Dead. Thomas Edison, a white man, caught the Thunder Beings and stuffed them in a glass bottle. White men fly in *this* world, in machines they make. My teacher says that if I study, I...*(LUCY turns to him; he breaks off. The two stand in silence for a moment.)* Why should I waste my life trapped on a reservation? To end up starving on top of a mountain like my grandfather? I don't...

(He breaks off as THE OLD MAN, wrapped in a buffalo robe, enters with the TWO RELATIVES; one carries the sacred pipe in an elaborately decorated leather pipe bag.)

LUCY. What else do they teach you at government school? *(HOKSILA stands silent. LUCY turns to her father.)* Tell this boy what you have learned in a lifetime at the "government's school." *(THE OLD MAN stares silently at HOKSILA, then turns away. He drops his buffalo robe and begins to remove the red paint from his body with the moist towel. With LUCY's assistance, he dresses in the shirt and suit that she has laid out.)* I'll tell you what I learned. Our religion: forbidden. Our language, our way of dancing: forbidden. Should we care? If we're to have danc- ing, if we're to have a purification, if we're to hear the story of The People, we have to hide in this place, back in the hills. If our ways still matter, you must speak of them, and of your great vision.

THE OLD MAN. Speak of the mission I have never fulfilled? Speak of a tree that should have flourished in our hearts but now is withered? Speak of a people who died in the blizzard...in the bloody snow? I do not wish to speak of this to children.

LUCY. Then who *will* speak to them? After you are gone, who will be left to speak to them? *(From off L, a GROUP OF PEOPLE is heard singing a Lakota song—the "En- couragement Song"—to the beat of hand-drums.)*

THE RELATIVES.
> *Lakol Oyate Kin Naji Yo*
> *Lakotapi Tehikelo Hey*
> *Inaji Yo Lakotapi Tehikelo*

THE OLD MAN. What is this singing? Lucy, what is this singing?

LUCY. Your relatives.

THE OLD MAN. What? Why are they here? Why are they singing?

LUCY. When you began your fast, the relatives gathered to hear you.

THE OLD MAN. Lucy, I will not speak of this.

LUCY. You must. If your vision was ever true and mighty, it...

THE OLD MAN. I cannot speak of...

LUCY *(quickly turns to HOKSILA)*. Sing. Sing with them.

HOKSILA *(proud of his decision)*. I don't speak Lakota. *(The off-stage singing ceases. Silence. THE OLD MAN is stunned. He crosses to HOKSILA and looks directly into his face. HOKSILA stares back without flinching.)* No one speaks Lakota anymore...except ghosts from the past. Lakota is history.

THE OLD MAN. The People without their history are no more than wind on the buffalo grass.

HOKSILA. I speak English. Civilized English.

THE OLD MAN. Yes, I must speak to this boy—to all of the children. Let them come. *(LUCY and the TWO MEN exit. THE OLD MAN turns his gaze back to HOKSILA.)*

HOKSILA. Grandfather, I...*(He offers the wooden bowl.)* Drink this.

THE OLD MAN. Where did you get this cup?

HOKSILA. It was by the well. *(THE OLD MAN looks at it carefully as his memory searches back almost sixty years.)*

THE OLD MAN. In my vision, the Grandfathers offered a wooden cup full of water; in the water was the sky. "Take this," the Voice said, "it is the power to make live, and it is yours."

HOKSILA. It's just a wooden cup; I filled it from the well! *(THE OLD MAN drinks from the cup.)*

SCENE 1B
A Ceremonial Ground in the Black Hills
October, 1931

(A new song erupts as two dozen of his RELATIVES rush into the space enclosed by the red hoop. They are excited—full of anticipation. Some are beating hand-drums; some are dancing. All ADULTS are singing a Lakota song—the "Entrance Song"; the CHILDREN and TEEN-AGERS are not. THE OLD MAN watches the children and the young adults closely.)

LAKOTA ADULTS.
> *Lakota Waste Wahielo*
> *Lakota Waci Oyate Leciya*
> *Waste Waci Wahielo*
> *Leciya Waste Waci Wahielo*
> *Wahielo*

(When the song ends, the RELATIVES sit in a circle just inside the red hoop. The circle is unbroken except for one space. A RELATIVE invites HOKSILA to sit in the open space, but the boy pushes rudely past and sits outside the circle. The RELATIVES adjust, closing the circle. THE OLD MAN places the cup on one of the rock ledges above the hoop and then joins the circle. He murmurs a ritual greeting in Lakota; his RELATIVES return the greeting. There is an expectant hush. The RELATIVES have come to participate in a "winter-telling," the foundation of the Oglala's oral tradition. They are dressed in very poor reservation clothes—shapeless and colorless government-issue sweaters and coats and other castoffs from the white world. Both men and women have long hair. It is worn a variety of ways—loose, braided, tied back, etc. As THE OLD MAN considers his task, he eyes the young people whose number stretches up to include the entire audience. He brings his gaze back to their parents.)

THE OLD MAN. I am going to tell you the story of my life, as you wish; if it were only the story of my life, I would not tell it, for what is one man that he should make much of his winters, even when they bend him like a heavy snow? It is a story of all life that is holy and is good to tell, and of us two-leggeds sharing in it with the four-leggeds and the wings of the air and all green things; for these are children of one mother and their father is one spirit. Is not the sky a father and the earth a mother? And are not all living things with feet or wings or roots their children? *(A murmur of assent moves through the RELATIVES.)* I was not born till The-Moon-of-Popping-Trees in The-Winter-When-Four-Crows-Were-Killed, December, 1863. You know me as Black Elk, a Medicine Man, a Lakota of our great Oglala Sioux. My father and his father before him bore this name, and the father of his father, so that I am the fourth to bear it. When I was young and could still hope, I heard a Voice call to me; the Voice was so beautiful nothing anywhere could keep from dancing. It said, "All over the Universe, they have finished a day of happiness; behold this day for it is yours to make." It said, "You shall stand upon the center of the world." And I asked where that might be, and the Voice said, "Anywhere is the center of the world." *(A murmur moves through the RELATIVES.)* And then...a vision was sent to me. In my vision, I reached the peak of the highest mountain in the Black Hills. Round about, beneath me, was the whole hoop of the world. From the rocks, colors flashed upward to become a rainbow in flame. From where I stood, I saw more than I can tell, and I understood more than I saw for I was seeing in a sacred manner. I saw that the sacred hoop of my people was one of many hoops that made one circle, and being endless, it was holy. *(BLACK ELK moves into the circle.)* I was told that it was my mission to place a bright red stick at the living center of the nation's hoop and to make that red stick grow into a tree; a shielding tree that would bloom, a mighty flowering tree to shelter the children, a tree to protect The People, to save us from the winds! *(His voice breaks.)* But the mighty vision was given to a man too weak to use it. There is no shelter for the children; the winds are fighting like gunfire, like whirling smoke, like women and children wailing, like horses screaming all over the world. The hoop that once held our lives is broken; our people, scattered with no center. And our children do not sing. These children do not know the greatness and truth of our tradition. We must teach them. We will do it together—an Indian pictograph in which you finally see what else was killed at Wounded Knee. Some of us will put on the war bonnets of our great Chiefs; some, the uniforms to try to look like the bluecoat soldiers, or like the "important men" who come out here to rearrange our lives. *(The REL-ATIVES laugh. BLACK ELK signals the drummers. They respond with a flourish.)* "The Winning of the West"...as experienced by the Indian People. *(On BLACK ELK's signal, several RELATIVES exit to change for their first winter-telling "roles." The FOUR DRUMMERS move UR and sing a Lakota melody— "Song Behind Black Elk." BLACK ELK and HOKSILA remain on stage throughout the play.)*

BLACK ELK. The old men say the earth, only, endures. They speak truly. They are right. And we are no more than names whispered by a wind rustling through a field of corn on a summer night—people who live in happiness and sorrow to become grass on these hills; and a few names on the maps—Sioux City, Pontiac, Miami, Lake Huron, Omaha. Before these road signs were posted to our memory, these were people! See them with me. See the great tribes of the East from where the light comes. See the Mohawk! The Pequot! The Narragansett!...

(As he says each name, the FOUR DRUMMERS respond with a flourish, and a CHIEF, wearing the best of his tribe's ceremonial attire, enters carrying an elaborate staff that is the symbol of his nation.)

BLACK ELK. To the South. The Cherokee! Seminole! Nav-
    ajo! See our neighbors, the Cheyenne! Our relatives, the
    Santee...and the Lakotas! See the great horse nation of the
    Sioux ride out across the unfenced prairie. Free men. *(The
    drums pound; MEN send war cries; the WOMEN send the
    tremolo and the LAKOTA CHIEF throws back his head
    and sends the piercing scream of an eagle. In the moment
    of quiet that follows, BLACK ELK admonishes softly.)* Our
    thoughts should rise high as eagles do. *(The RELATIVES
    who represent the NINE CHIEFS form an elaborate tab-
    leau on the levels above the circle. The splendor of their
    native dress is a vivid contrast with the reservation wear of
    BLACK ELK and the RELATIVES still sitting in the winter-
    telling circle. LUCY gives BLACK ELK an elaborately-
    carved wooden mask decorated with bone, feathers, leather
    and metal.)* Somewhere up in the winds Chief Tecumseh
    still speaks to us. Words that still haunt us. *(He holds the
    huge mask of Chief Tecumseh above his head to create a
    figure ten feet tall; the words of the chief flow through
    him.)* Sleep not longer, O my brothers. Think not you can
    remain passive to the common danger and escape the com-
    mon fate or we will vanish before the greed and oppression
    of the white man as snow before the summer sun. Shall we
    let the white man cut down our trees to build fences around
    us? Shall we give up our homes, our country bequeathed to
    us by the Great Spirit, the graves of our dead and every-
    thing that is dear and sacred to us? I know you will cry
    with me...Never!

ALL. NEVER! *(The CHIEFS disperse muttering eight dimin-
    ishing "Nevers." Five of the ceremonial staffs are left
    planted in the ground. The FOUR DRUMMERS move UC
    to a recess under the wooden platforms. They remain on
    stage throughout the performance to sing and play a vari-*

ety of native and wasichu instruments. Several RELATIVES also remain, sitting in a circle just inside the hoop.)

BLACK ELK. If you are to understand the ending in the blizzard, you must know the beginning in the warm waters off a tropical island on which our cousins, the Tainos, are about to discover Columbus. *(BLACK ELK tosses a blanket to a RELATIVE who still sits in the circle wearing wasichu clothing.)* Arrange this blanket like a Columbus robe. You will be the Priest! *(He hands a cross to a RELATIVE, also in wasichu clothing. Speaks to the RELATIVE PLAYING COLUMBUS, who has wrapped the blanket around himself in a way worn by the Indians.)* No, to look like Columbus! Good! His crew had mutinied. They were about to turn back; then the lookout saw something in the water...*(Incredulous at the irony.)*...a branch from a tree in flower.

THE PRIEST. *Terra! Terra firma!*

THE RELATIVE WHO PLAYS COLUMBUS *(clowning to cover his embarrassment with a first foray into "acting").* Mama Mia! Look at all the redskins! *(The RELATIVES laugh.)*

BLACK ELK *(furious).* No, no. Columbus was a great chief. Within your mind, you must see the true picture. With your mind you must make him real.

SCENE 2A
The Eastern Shore of San Salvador
October 12, 1492

(The RELATIVE who plays COLUMBUS murmurs an apology and concentrates; the DRUMMERS begin to sing—the "Taino Friendship Song"—accompanied by a wooden drum and a rain stick.)

MUSICIANS.

> *Gwai Tiow Gua-re-koh Ah-ru Wa Ka-gwa Ki-ah*
> *Gwai Tiow Gua-re-koh Ah-ru Wa Ka-gwa Ki-ah*
> *Gwai Tiow Gua-re-koh Ah-ru Wa Ka-gwa Ki-ah*
> *Gwai Tiow Gua-re-koh Ah-ru Wa Ka-gwa Ki-ah*

(Warm, tropical lights meet FOUR TAINOS as they enter. They are curious, friendly and almost naked. The TAINO CHIEF carries his nation's staff which is encrusted with sea shells and decorated with feathers, a turtle shell and pieces of hammered gold. The TAINOS move inside the winter-telling circle bearing ceremonial gifts of fish, shellfish, tropical fruits and flowers. This "pre-Columbian" scene is natural and beautiful—the Christian parallel of the "Garden of Eden." COLUMBUS and the PRIEST speak with the accent of first generation Italian immigrants heard on the streets of New York in 1931. COLUMBUS is about to give the native inhabitants of this new world a name.)

COLUMBUS. These...these...what shall we call them? Indios?

PRIEST. Indios!

COLUMBUS *(to the PRIEST)*. I ask you to forgive their nakedness, which is only from ignorance. These Indios are a gentle people, without fraud or malice. They believe we come from the sky. *(The TAINOS present their gifts; the PRIEST pushes his cross forward as though to ward off the devil.)*

BLACK ELK. Not from the sky. Our ancestors told us, "Men with hairy faces will come from the east like the light of dawn."

PRIEST. You have been delivered to our faith by love. Kneel. Kneel.

COLUMBUS. They don't understand. Unfortunately they are not a practical people...existing simply as you see, gathering wild fruit and mollusks. We must teach them to work, clear land, do all that is part of the natural order.

BLACK ELK. We were wrong about the dawn. They came like the night and we began to die.

THE RELATIVE WHO PLAYS COLUMBUS. Not before you had been baptized.

COLUMBUS *(taking the cross from the PRIEST and extending it to the TAINOS).* We bring you hope for Heaven.

PRIEST. Wait...redskinned people are not mentioned in the Bible; this raises a serious question as to whether or not they are actually human beings.

COLUMBUS. Personally, I am convinced they are human... even though they are unnaturally generous. Some would say, irresponsible! Let me show you. *(He points to one of the TAINOS, a YOUNG WOMAN.)* You. Yes, you. I admire that ornament on your arm. *(She follows his gestures and touches her bracelet.)* Yes, that's it. *(Without hesitation she takes off her bracelet and proudly gifts it to CO-LUMBUS.)* Charming. Thank you, child. There! You see!

BLACK ELK. At the time it seemed such a trifle. *(COLUMBUS and THE PRIEST examine the bracelet.)*

COLUMBUS. Quite malleable, no alloys.

BLACK ELK. If there was ever any hope for us, *this* was the moment in which it was lost.

COLUMBUS. Gold! *(COLUMBUS and the PRIEST turn a new-found interest to the body decorations worn by the TAINOS. They rush into the welcoming party, snatch the staff from the TAINO CHIEF and claw at its gold ornaments. The TAINOS pick up their valuable gifts of food and again offer them as they frantically sing their friendship song. As the WASICHUS [the Lakota word for white people] fight over the staff, they break it in half, toss the broken parts aside and rush off waving their new-found treasures above their heads.)*

COLUMBUS and the PRIEST. Gold! Gold! Gold! *(A RELATIVE moves into the winter-telling circle and begins to swing a carved piece of wood on the end of a leather thong. This is a native wind-whistle which, when vigorously twirled in a six-foot arc, creates the howling sound of a blizzard. This powerful wind blows the TAINOS offstage.)*

SCENE 2B
Washington, D.C., May, 1830

BLACK ELK. The cold winds that gathered in the islands begin blowing out across the many lands of the people. *(The DRUMMERS replace the Taino song with "Yankee Doodle" sung in the same rhythmic structure to the beat of the wooden Taino drum.)*

MUSICIANS.

    Yankee Doodle went to town
    A-riding on a pony,
    Stuck a feather in his hat
    and called it macaroni.

    Yankee Doodle keep it up
    Yankee Doodle dandy...

(In a choreographed sequence, three RELATIVES playing WASICHUS enter UC over the ridge. One is a pilgrim, one an Indian fighter [Daniel Boone] and one a Colonial sol-

dier. They attack the forest of staffs planted by the chiefs, destroying the staffs of the Seminole, the Mohawks, the Pequots, and the Narragansetts. They toss the broken parts on top of the shattered Taino staff. This creates a junk-pile; the Colonial soldier produces a thirteen-star American flag and the group forms an heroic tableau above the junk-pile. The wind-whistle screams as the RELATIVE circles the tableau.)

BLACK ELK. White people colonies now cover the land near the big water to the East. We discover that a prominent Indian killer has been elected their president. We call him Sharp Knife.

(The RELATIVE who will play ANDREW JACKSON enters, draws his sword and cuts the Cherokee staff in half. The wind-whistle stops.)

BLACK ELK. They call him Andrew Jackson. *(JACKSON tosses the pieces of the Cherokee staff onto the junk-pile, sheaths his sword and comes forward. If one ignores his native face and long braids, and concentrates on his sword, sash, shirt and bicorn hat, he looks like the seventh president of the United States... or a pirate.)*

(A RELATIVE enters with a lectern made from buckskin stretched over a frame of sticks; he places it in front of the pile of broken staffs and sits in the circle to watch. The Presidential Seal is painted on the front of the lectern. Standing in the pile of broken staffs and backed by the flag and the FOUR WASICHUS, JACKSON speaks in the Scottish accent of his parents to an unseen audience of "whites" from America's "bully pulpit.")

JACKSON. To prevent racial incidents between the citizens of Georgia and the Cherokee, I suggest the propriety of removing the Indians, for their own good, removing them west of the Mississippi where they'll enjoy the protection of a permanent Indian frontier which I promise for as long as grass grows and water runs.

BLACK ELK *(to "the children")*. It will not be the grass or the water that forgets. Mr. President. You made us so many promises, but you kept only one—you promised to take our land, and you took it.

JACKSON. You cannot blame us with the reality that grows out of the inevitable march of human events. It is our manifest destiny to possess this land.

BLACK ELK. What is it? What is it that drives you crazy? The yellow metal?

JACKSON. What would Indians do with gold?

BLACK ELK. Nothing!

JACKSON *(to his unseen "white" constituents)*. There! You see.

BLACK ELK. I only see your special way with words. When you steal land, you call it "Manifest Destiny." If an Indian tries to defend himself, you call him "a hostile." After destroying us with guns, whiskey and smallpox, you say, "we've vanished"...

JACKSON. It is our manifest destiny. *(Led by the RELATIVE with the wind-whistle who sends ill-winds before them, JACKSON takes the flag from the Colonial soldier and, followed by the other WASICHUS, marches off. As they exit, they sing:)*

THE DRUMMERS and the FIVE WASICHUS.
> My country tis of thee,
> Sweet land of liberty...

BLACK ELK *(turning quickly to HOKSILA, his shout inter-*
rupts the singing). Some things will *not* vanish. To the
south our cousins, the Navajo, elect a new chief,
Manuelito. *(The big drum roars. Several RELATIVES*
gather the "bully pulpit," the Taino's gifts, and the broken
staffs and push the pieces off the edges of the stage. The
broken staffs do not disappear; they protrude into
sightlines. These images of Peoples destroyed will grow
throughout the performance until the entire stage seems to
rest on a junk-pile of Indian Nations.)

SCENE 3A
In and Around Fort Wingate, New Mexico Territory
September 22, 1861

(As the stage is cleared, the RELATIVE who will play
MANUELITO enters with the staff of the Navajo Nation.
The staff is topped by branches of peach trees springing
from the skull of a ram with its large curved horns still
intact. Corn, wool, turquoise, silver and basketwork are
prominently featured decorations on the staff.
MANUELITO strides forward and plants his staff in the
winter-telling circle. MANUELITO, a Navajo War Chief, is
a large muscular man of great energy and a wonderful
ironic sense of humor. He wears classic Navajo pants and
leggings; his upper torso is naked except for magnificent
silver and turquoise jewelry; across his right shoulder is
an intricately woven woolen blanket; on his head, a
brightly-colored headband. HE is followed by a CLOWN
SPIRIT who walks on all fours by using ritual sticks to
extend each arm. The SPIRIT's body and face are painted
white with dark blue features drawn on the face.)

THE RELATIVE WHO PLAYS MANUELITO. In a sacred manner I live. My horses are many. *(With great good humor.)* My wives are also numerous. My mules...more than you could count! *(The best of all.)* And my peach tree orchards! *Five thousand peach trees! Blooming in the desert!* Men call me Manuelito of the Navajo. We capture mules from the Mexicans. This began because the Mexicans capture children from us to sell as slaves. And when we go to reclaim our children, we gather up all the livestock in sight. This is so logical! Then the Americans came and they complicated everything. They named our land New Mexico, and the Mexicans became American citizens. This does not stop them from stealing Navajo children, but now when we retaliate, American soldiers chase after us because we are not citizens. We could not become American citizens, because we are Indians. Do you follow that? I don't follow that!

They built this Fort Defiance and they wrote down many promises and said we must keep the promises. And we kept the promises. Then some of our cattle strayed. We cannot help that. But the soldiers rode out and shot them. Then they started burning our hogans. This is where we live. I assembled a force of a thousand warriors and just before dawn we attacked this Fort Defiance. We burned some buildings and got them so confused, they started shooting each other. At daylight we pulled back into our hills. A magnificent demonstration! You cannot imagine how seriously this was taken by the United States army. They sent companies of cavalry to scour the mountains for "the hostiles." But when they tried to corner us in our own mountains, they accomplished only one thing, they exhausted their horses. *(With an amused shrug.)* So, finally they made peace. Now when we go to the fort, it is to trade, and for *horse races! (A festive swirl. The DRUM-MERS sing the "Tineh Gambling Song.")*

MUSICIANS.

>*Hey nik-eh tee Hey wah na-ah*
>*Hey nik-eh tee Hey wah na*
>*Ha 'tse mah-nah Hey wah na*
>*Ha 'tse mah-na Hey wah na*

(Throughout the song the RELATIVES watching from the winter-telling circle stand and become NAVAJO by adding blankets. Other NAVAJO join them from R. The RELATIVES who will play SOLDIERS enter L. One of the SOLDIERS carries a U.S. Flag. [The soldiers' uniforms are Lakota war shirts with the buckskin painted blue and the fringe and army insignias painted gold. Each uniform is topped by either a cavalry cap for an enlisted man, or a felt hat for an officer. Under the shirts, each relative wears Lakota breechclout and leggings. The visual reference for all costumes except "reservation wear" can be found in Lakota pictographs.] The CORPORAL strides up to YOUNG NAVAJO. Music ends.)

CORPORAL. Hey! Bet ya a dollar agin your blanket.

MANUELITO *(as he places his own blanket on the YOUNG NAVAJO's shoulder).* Three dollars against this blanket!

CORPORAL. You've got a bet. No Navajo pony kin beat a quarter horse.

YOUNG NAVAJO. Quarter horses don't last. We bet on the pony.

CORPORAL. You don't have a chance. Our best horse will be ridden by Lieutenant *Ortiz. (Shout of approval from the*

SOLDIERS as ORTIZ prances into the focus on his horse-dance stick.)

MANUELITO. But *our* best horse will be ridden by *ME! MANUELITO! (NAVAJO pandemonium, shouts. MANUEL-ITO is handed a horse-dance stick by a NAVAJO. The TWO RIDERS move their "mounts" to the starting line.)* On your mark, get set...(*The CORPORAL points a rifle into the sky and fires to signal the start of the race. [The sound of the rifle is made by the strike of a drum. All gun shots in the production are created by the drummers.] The DRUMMERS and NAVAJOS dance, sing and shout a Lakota Horse Song in a choreographed ritual. The Navajo staff is used as a rallying standard for the NAVAJO; the U.S. flag is used as a rallying standard for the SOLDIERS.)*

MUSICIANS and NAVAJOS.

> *Sunka wakan mani ko-ke-pop-ay-lo*
> *Sunka wakan mani ko-ke-pop-ay-lo*
> *Sunka wakan mani ko-ke-pop-ay-lo Hey-hey Hey-hey*
> *Sunka wakan mani ko-ke-pop-ay-lo Hey-oy*

(At first, ORTIZ's quarter-horse breaks into the lead, but the Navajo pony overtakes and passes him. On the final turn, the Navajo pony begins to spin out of control and carries MANUELITO off the race course. ORTIZ's quar-ter-horse rounds the turn and crosses the finish line. The choreographed sequence is over. The NAVAJO are stunned. The SOLDIERS are loud and derisive. Music ends.)

SOLDIER. We win, we win! Whipped him good!

CORPORAL. The Chief can't even handle his pony!

LIEUTENANT ORTIZ. Indians can't stand competition, just come apart, got no grit, none of 'em!

CORPORAL. Pay up!

MANUELITO *(with the remnants of a leather bridle).* Some soldier bet more than he could afford? Is that why he slashed my bridle? *(The CLOWN SPIRIT sends the sound of the owl to warn MANUELITO.)*

LIEUTENANT ORTIZ. Come on, back to the fort.

YOUNG NAVAJO. Wait! His bridle was cut! See for yourself!

CORPORAL. We already seen, and you lost! *(The CORPORAL jerks Manuelito's blanket from the YOUNG NAVAJO's shoulder.)*

YOUNG NAVAJO. You cheated! Give back the blanket!

MANUELITO. It does not matter. Let him take it!

CORPORAL. Was you thinkin' he might stop me? You thievin' Navajo kin always steal somethin' else...*(The SOLDIERS exit over the ridge.)*

YOUNG NAVAJO. Run the race over! Come back and run an honest race! Bluecoat dogs! *(Racing after the SOLDIERS.)* Cowards! Cowar...*(A rifle shot cuts him short. He falls backwards and tumbles down the ridge to the edge of the hoop. For a moment the NAVAJO are frozen with horror.)*

MANUELITO. Get the children, get on your ponies, get out! Quickly! Get mounted! Get to the hills! *(WOMEN search frantically for CHILDREN; there are whimpers of fear and cries of fright. More shots are fired and the NAVAJO scatter, running, trying to collect each other and get out.)* Get away! This way, GO! *(The massacre is choreographed to a flurry of drums. It ends with several NAVAJO dead. BLACK ELK walks to the center of the group of bodies and offering his hand to one of the women, he helps the DEAD to rise.)*

BLACK ELK *(quips)*. After this we had some unexpected good luck. The graycoat soldiers and the bluecoat soldiers started killing each other. Like many nice things, it did not last. *(The RELATIVES sit in the winter-telling circle.)*

SCENE 3B
Santa Fe, New Mexico Territory, Spring 1862

(A RELATIVE begins to twirl a wind-whistle. As the wind howls, the RELATIVE who will play GENERAL CARLE-TON enters carrying an elaborate strongbox painted in the blue and gold of the U.S. Cavalry. The box is topped by the bald eagle symbol of the U.S.A., and has the letters "U.S." emblazoned on the side. It is secured by a hasp and a large gold padlock. CARLETON's long leather coat is painted blue with gold stars. He is followed by an AIDE who carries a small table. The AIDE places the table inside the winter-telling circle, CARLETON puts the strong-box on it, pulls a telescope from his pocket and begins to search the horizon.)

BLACK ELK. After all the graycoats had been killed or driven away, more and more bluecoats kept coming into our country, an army of bluecoats under General Carleton. He began looking for someone else to kill. *(CARLETON's spyglass focuses on MANUELITO; the CLOWN SPIRIT sounds a warning and quickly moves to protect MANUEL-ITO. CARLETON speaks in a French accent.)*

GENERAL CARLETON. As Commanding General, I'm concerned with the future of this great pastoral region, this princely realm.

MANUELITO. Thank you.

GENERAL CARLETON. Unfortunately this valuable tract is infested with Indians, Navajo. You people are wolves...

BLACK ELK. Would you like to guess just who he is deciding to kill?

GENERAL CARLETON. ...you must be removed and confined on lands our president...uh, the great White Father, has set aside for you: the Bosque Redondo. *(The CLOWN SPIRIT sounds his warning.)*

MANUELITO. The Bosque Redondo? You want to force *people* onto land so dry it won't grow corn or feed sheep?

GENERAL CARLETON *(the answer is obvious)*. We must open this land for American citizens.

MANUELITO. There are people already on this land.

GENERAL CARLETON. You're not citizens.

MANUELITO. The Navajo have lived in these mountains for more generations than anyone can count.

GENERAL CARLETON. You're not citizens. You will be moved.

MANUELITO. If you cage the badger, he'll fight to break free. Chain the eagle, and he'll struggle with fury to regain the sky, which is *his* home.

GENERAL CARLETON *(to his AIDE)*. Effective immediately: there shall be no council held with the Indians.

CARLETON'S AIDE. Yes sir.

GENERAL CARLETON *(to MANUELITO)*. Unless you go to the Bosque Redondo, your men will be killed wherever found.

BLACK ELK. Not much room for negotiation! *(CARLETON signals. The AIDE moves the table with the strongbox to the Navajo staff.)*

THE RELATIVE WHO PLAYS MANUELITO. General Carleton ordered his soldiers to destroy our fields. Can you understand this? Destroying the earth with its pastures, corn, the beautiful peach trees. These raids, their purpose was starvation. Can you follow that? I can't follow that. *(A flurry of gunfire is heard. MANUELITO drops to the floor to hide. CARLETON crosses to the table, takes out a key, unlocks the strongbox and takes out a pair of scissors.*

Using his sticks, the CLOWN SPIRIT lifts MANUELITO to his feet.)

GENERAL CARLETON. You face a superior force. You have no food. You cannot win. Go to the Bosque Redondo.

MANUELITO. We will stay on our land! On the burned-out remains of our land!

GENERAL CARLETON. The war will be pursued until your people cease to exist. *(CARLETON snips the decorations from the Navajo staff and drops them into the strongbox. He signals the AIDE who moves the U.S. flag to the UR exit. The NAVAJO begin to desert MANUELITO and tip-toe UR to disappear behind the flag.)*

MANUELITO. The People will stay. And The People will live! We will never be driven away. We will never submit. We were born in the Chuska mountains; we will remain in the Chuska mountains. Our God lives here. We will never...*(A NAVAJO WOMAN carrying a CHILD rises from the winter-telling circle and starts to join the REFUGEES. MANUELITO turns to look at her.)* Where do you go?

NAVAJO WOMAN. To turn ourselves in. To be sent to the Bosque Redondo.

MANUELITO. Do you know about the Bosque? *(Silence.)* The soldiers run you through a pen gate like sheep, so you can be counted. For shelter you clear out a burrow in the ground where you will live like the coyote. Could any fate be worse?

NAVAJO WOMAN. Watching my children starve to death. Can you protect your women? Can you feed your children? Then come with us to the Bosque.

MANUELITO. I will not move from our mountains.

NAVAJO WOMAN. Your grave is already made.

The Long Walk.
March, April and May, 1864

(A native flute cries softly— "Navajo March to Bosque"—
as the REFUGEES, carrying possessions on their backs
and heads, begin the Long Walk. Led by CARLETON's
AIDE with the flag, the procession appears on top of the
ridge UR and proceeds across the stage in a counter-
clockwise circle. The endless procession continues for sev-
eral minutes. As it grinds on, exhaustion and sickness force
the NAVAJO to abandon their possessions. By the end,
they have almost nothing; those that have the strength
struggle to carry their weaker relatives. CARLETON con-
tinues to "prune" the Navajo staff.)

BLACK ELK. It is the Moon of the Strong Cold as they start
     their 400-mile walk to the Bosque. Soldiers mistreat them.
     Children are snatched from their mothers to be sold as
     slaves. The food they are given is flour which The People
     do not know how to prepare. They mix the flour with
     water and try to eat the cold paste. And they walk, people
     with empty eyes; and as they walk, they think about their
     home in the mountains, flocks feeding in valley pastures,
     the smell of piñon smoke from their campfires, eagles
     sweeping across the sky. And they start to die. Even the
     New Mexicans are beginning to talk of the bad ways of
     Star Chief Carleton. *(To GENERAL CARLETON.)* But you
     are too busy to listen; too busy leading your regiment
     against less than twenty ragged, starving...
GENERAL CARLETON *(the final description).* Hostiles!
MANUELITO *(with angry agreement).* HOSTILES! *(The*
     procession halts and the flute pauses.)
GENERAL CARLETON. Throw down your weapons.

MANUELITO. Weapons? If we had weapons, we would not go to the Bosque. If we had weapons, we would use them!

September 1866

(Flute resumes. MANUELITO pulls one of the exhausted men to his feet and joins the line of refugees; the PROCESSION resumes. CARLETON carefully locks the strongbox and then pulls the remains of the Navajo staff from the ground and shoves it into the junk-pile.)

GENERAL CARLETON. The exodus of this whole people from the land of their fathers is not only an interesting but a touching sight. They fought us gallantly; they defended their mountains with heroism of which any people might be proud until they found it was their destiny, as it has been the destiny of their brethren, tribe after tribe, to give way to the preordained progress of civilization!

(The last of the REFUGEES exits; the music stops; there is a moment of empty silence. To the sound of a rattle, the AIDE enters and gives CARLETON an important looking document. CARLETON opens it and reads.)

BLACK ELK. There should be a special page in this history called "The-Time-Three-Right-Things-Were-Done." The first, removing an oppressive general.

GENERAL CARLETON. I...I...I've been removed from this command!? For what reason? Eighteen days after I forced the surrender of the Hostiles? I opened this land for us, our claims, for our settlement, this princely realm!

(As he exits, the RELATIVE who will play NORTON, en-ters.)

BLACK ELK. The second right thing, appointing a humane man as superintendent of an Indian reservation. His name should be remembered. It was Norton. A. Baldwin Norton.

The Bosque Redondo, New Mexico Territory
February 17, 1867

(NORTON, a young man just graduated from an Ivy League school, wears thick glasses and carries a briefcase. He speaks with a Boston accent.)

NORTON. Why would any sensible man select the Bosque Redondo for a reservation? The water is brackish, the soil is poor and cold, and the mesquite roots, twelve miles dis-tant, are the only wood for the Indians to use. If they re-main on this reservation, they must always be held by force and not from choice. Let them go back—back to where they can have good cool water to drink, enough wood to keep them from freezing to death, and where the soil will produce something for them to eat!

BLACK ELK. Now we come to the biggest miracle of all—someone heard this man! Officials came from what we call "The-Place-Where-Everything-Is-Disputed." Others call it "Washington." *(NORTON exits. The NAVAJO REFUGEES crowd behind wooden bars that block the R entrance.)* These officials held many councils with the Navajo. The Navajo agreed and agreed and agreed to the new treaty, if they could just go home. Then...

MANUELITO. It is time; time to load the wagons. *(Shout-ing.)* Time to move out! *Now!*

SCENE 3C
The Return, New Mexico Territory, June 18, 1868

(The bars are torn away and cries explode from the waiting NAVAJO; drums beat as they race around and around the hoop. When the big drum sounds an honor beat, the RETURNING NAVAJO spread across the space enclosed by the hoop and shout to the hills and the sky. Some of the old men and women cry; they sink to their knees, talk to the earth and rub its rich soil on their faces and bodies. The CLOWN SPIRIT rises out of the junk-pile with the charred remains of the Navajo staff; a single new ear of corn provides its only color. An ELDER NAVAJO stands and begins to sing. One by one, the others stand to join the song until it reverberates from the hills.)

NAVAJO and MUSICIANS.
>*She-na-sha She-na-sha*
>*She-na-sha She-na-sha*
>*Bic-kay hozjo-nah ay ya hay nay-yah*
>*Ah-kah-la Ah-kah-la, gon-nah-sha*
>*Ah-kah-la Ah-kah-la, gon-nah-sha*

(The CLOWN SPIRIT proudly carries the beginnings of a new Navajo staff UC, mounts the ledge, climbs up the ridge towards the Chuska mountains and disappears UR. BLACK ELK softly speaks the words of the song as the Navajo hum the first two phrases of the tune, repeating as needed. Music ends on the word "earth.")

BLACK ELK.
>In beauty we walk
>There is beauty around me

There is beauty above me

There is beauty in the earth

(To HOKSILA.) The Navajo had come home.

HOKSILA *(a cynic).* Home? A tiny burned-out remnant of their land? Charred peach trees that will never flower again?

THE RELATIVE WHO PLAYED MANUELITO. But we survived! The People will live!

HOKSILA. The People won't "live" unless they face reality. We lost the war! We can wither in the desert, hiding from the Twentieth Century, or we can learn their way, live their way and prosper their way.

BLACK ELK *(to HOKSILA).* Give me your coat.

HOKSILA. What?

BLACK ELK. For the story, I need your coat.

HOKSILA. Why?

BLACK ELK *(wryly).* To "face reality."

(HOKSILA takes off his coat and hands it to BLACK ELK. A RELATIVE spinning a wind-whistle enters UR. TWO RELATIVES remove Navajo shirts and sit in the winter-telling circle. All other RELATIVES exit.)

SCENE 4A
Santee Reservation, Minnesota, August, 1862

(As the blizzard howls, BLACK ELK points to TWO RELA-TIVES entering UL; when HOKSILA turns, he sees A REL-ATIVE wearing a U.S. army officer's uniform walking with a RELATIVE dressed as a SANTEE CHIEF. The CHIEF's war-bonnet is topped by the horns of an antelope with an

eagle feather trailer falling to the ground. He is naked above his breechclout and leggings. The SANTEE CHIEF plants the staff of the Santee Nation inside the winter-telling circle. The wind-whistles stop. The RELATIVE who will play WOWINAPA, the son of Little Crow, enters. WOWINAPA carries a war bonnet display pole which he pushes into the ground next to the Santee staff.)

BLACK ELK *(to HOKSILA)*. The cold winds that will finally pile up the snow over the crooked gulch at Wounded Knee are blowing across the Minnesota grasslands where our cousins, the Santee, guard our eastern frontier. *(The OFFI-CER presents a brass medal suspended from a colorful ribbon to the CHIEF. The CHIEF fastens the ribbon around his neck and then pulls beaver and ermine pelts from the Santee staff and presents them to the OFFICER. The TWO shake hands cordially and the OFFICER exits.)* We do not yet know that they have already been confined on a reservation like the Bosque. Where there are no buffalo, no food; the young men of the Santee blame their chief.

A VOICE *(from off)*. *Kangi' ci' k'ala* is a coward!

BLACK ELK. "*Kangi' ci' k'ala*" is the name of their chief who is also called "Little Crow."

VOICE *(from off)*. *Kangi' ci' k'ala* is a coward!

BLACK ELK. He is *called* coward, but he is not a coward. However, he has a quality often mistaken for cowardice... realism. The worst reality for Little Crow is that he touched the pen to the treaties that deceived his people. *(BLACK ELK hands HOKSILA's coat to WOWINAPA. LITTLE CROW removes his war bonnet and places it on the display pole.)*

WOWINAPA. Your new white-man coat, Father. *(LITTLE CROW exchanges his war bonnet for HOKSILA's coat.)*

LITTLE CROW. I cannot find a way to deal with them, these power-hungry men who always tell lies. It will help if I can appear more like them. *(He puts on HOKSILA's coat.)*

BLACK ELK *(to HOKSILA)*. Little Crow also built a small white-man house; and joined the Episcopal Church. *(The RELATIVES who will play SHAKOPEE and the SANTEE ELDER sit to form a tribal council; LITTLE CROW joins them. WOWINAPA stands above the council to listen.)*

VOICE *(from off)*. *Kangi' ci' k'ala* is a coward!

SHAKOPEE. What good does it do to wear the white-man coat?

SANTEE ELDER. What good did it do to go to Washington?

LITTLE CROW. I went to Washington to seek assistance from the "Great White Father" which is how Indians are expected to address President Buchanan.

SANTEE ELDER. Achieving what?

LITTLE CROW. President Buchanan assured me they will honor the treaty.

SHAKOPEE. When? Our people are starving. There is no buffalo left here; I am taking a hunting party to our old hunting grounds.

LITTLE CROW. No. We must also honor the treaty.

SANTEE ELDER. Our children cannot eat the treaty.

LITTLE CROW. The treaty provides for annuities.

SHAKOPEE. What annuities? I've seen no...

LITTLE CROW. The *payments* are called annuities. When the payments come, we'll exchange the money for food.

SHAKOPEE. Let's take the food now, and they can keep the annuities.

LITTLE CROW. That's not the way it's done. You're very ignorant of these things.

SHAKOPEE. My stomach is especially ignorant.

LITTLE CROW. We must honor the treaty!

A VOICE *(from off)*. *Kangi' ci' k'ala* is a coward! *(LITTLE CROW rises to signal the council is over.)*

LITTLE CROW. Honor the treaty or elect another to speak for you.

SHAKOPEE. It is under discussion.

LITTLE CROW *(stung)*. When I no longer have the responsibility, I will enjoy "discussion" too. I look forward to uncomplicated "discussions" of how great heroes should deal with our problems.

SHAKOPEE *(also stung)*. What we discuss is electing Traveling Hail to speak for us.

LITTLE CROW *(carefully)*. Traveling Hail would be an excellent spokesman.

SHAKOPEE. Meanwhile you have the responsibility. What will you do about your responsibility?

LITTLE CROW *(pauses. Frankly)*. Everything I can.

SCENE 4B
The Indian Agency Near Fort Ridgley, Minnesota
August 15, 1862

(TWO RELATIVES spin wind-whistles. The RELATIVE who will play THOMAS GALBRAITH, head of the Indian Agency, enters with a small table and stool which he places to the left side of the hoop. The RELATIVE who plays LONG TRADER SIBLEY enters with a small store counter which he places to the right side of the hoop. All of the SANTEE form a line and one at a time go to GALBRAITH who tears a printed I.O.U. from a four-inch wide roll of red tape, hands the I.O.U. to the SANTEE who then stands in line to present the I.O.U. to LONG TRADER SIBLEY who refuses to accept it. The SANTEE repeat the

useless process again and again. As the process grinds on
LITTLE CROW tries to speak with GALBRAITH who an-
swers in a Scottish accent.)

SIBLEY. No credit.

GALBRAITH. Move on.

SIBLEY. No credit.

GALBRAITH. Move on.

SIBLEY. Furs or cash; no credit!

GALBRAITH. Move on!

LITTLE CROW. Agent Galbraith! *(Wind-whistles out.)* Agent
Galbraith.

GALBRAITH. All they do is bellyache.

LITTLE CROW. We must talk about the annuities.

GALBRAITH. What made you think of annuities?

LITTLE CROW. Long Trader Sibley has opened his trading
post for business. I thought perhaps he smelled a little
money.

GALBRAITH. The money hasn't come. *(GALBRAITH offers*
LITTLE CROW an I.O.U. LITTLE CROW refuses.)

LITTLE CROW. This paper promise will not buy food. Annuities were pledged by the treaties; we must have them to
exchange for food.

GALBRAITH. The Great Council in Washington...

LITTLE CROW. The Congress.

GALBRAITH. The Great Congress in Washington has many
more important...

LITTLE CROW. Then give back our hunting grounds and
we'll say no more about it.

GALBRAITH *(the WASICHU roars with laughter).* Listen to
the Indian giver! You sold that land to U.S. citizens.

LITTLE CROW. Then where is the money? We have no
food, but here are warehouses filled with food. We ask that

you, as head of the Indian Agency, make some arrangement by which we can get something to eat from these warehouses.

GALBRAITH. I can't issue food before the arrival of the funds.

LITTLE CROW *(frantic with frustration)*. What are my people to eat while we wait?

GALBRAITH. As far as I'm concerned, eat grass! *(GAILBRAITH and SIBLEY pick up their furniture and exit. There's a moment of stunned silence; then the frustration of the SANTEE boils into rage.)*

THE SANTEE *(simultaneously)*. Grass! Break into the warehouses! Take the food! It's our food! Take our food and burn their buildings!

SHAKOPEE *(climaxing outburst)*. WAR!

LITTLE CROW. Wait!

SANTEE WOMAN. No! He's right.

LITTLE CROW *(a cry)*. He is not right! War? This is foolish talk!

SHAKOPEE. It is more foolish to starve.

LITTLE CROW. You do not realize their power. You have no idea. To fight a war against such power as they...

SHAKOPEE. Is this all you can say?

LITTLE CROW. I say, no war!

SHAKOPEE *(outraged)*. We need someone else to speak for us. *(The SANTEE push past LITTLE CROW and exit.)*

LITTLE CROW *(trying to reason with them)*. I have been to their land in the east, seen their giant forces, their terrible guns...

SHAKOPEE. Someone else! *(They've gone, leaving LITTLE CROW rejected and alone. A MUSICIAN plays a mournful flute—the "Santee Moon Song"; the lights dim slowly. WOWINAPA unrolls a buffalo robe. LITTLE CROW joins him; BOTH MEN prepare to sleep on the robe.)*

SCENE 4C
Santee Reservation, Minnesota, August 17, 1862

(A SPIRIT GUIDE emerges and moves to LITTLE CROW. The SPIRIT GUIDE is naked except for breechclout and moccasins; his body is painted with dark blue symbols; he wears the blue-black headdress of a crow. The SPIRIT GUIDE startles WOWINAPA by sending a warning with a buffalo horn rattle.)

WOWINAPA. Father, I...

LITTLE CROW. It is not our concern. Go to sleep. *(The SPIRIT GUIDE sounds the rattle again. WOWINAPA starts.)*

LITTLE CROW. Please...get some rest.

(LITTLE CROW and WOWINAPA lie down to sleep. Silhouetted against the sky, FOUR RELATIVES dressed for a HUNTING PARTY enter. The HUNTERS include SHAKOPEE and MEDICINE BOTTLE. They are whispering in low anxious voices.)

WOWINAPA. Father...

LITTLE CROW *(getting up)*. I know. I doubt very much they're coming to wake us with good news. *(The SPIRIT GUIDE sounds the warning rattle. Calling to the nighttime visitors.)* Why are you here?

SHAKOPEE. Some young men of my band were hungry. We crossed the river to hunt in the Big Woods, because we were very hungry. *(The SPIRIT GUIDE sounds the rattle again.)*

LITTLE CROW. Go on.

SHAKOPEE. Something happened.

MEDICINE BOTTLE. We came to a settler's fence; I found a hen's nest with some eggs.

SHAKOPEE. I warned him, don't take the eggs...

MEDICINE BOTTLE *(with contempt).* ...they belong to the white man.

SHAKOPEE. He called me a coward! *(The SPIRIT GUIDE sounds a sustained rattle.)*

LITTLE CROW. And what did you do to prove you are not a coward?

SHAKOPEE. I asked if he was brave enough to go up to the house with me while I shot the white man. He said...

MEDICINE BOTTLE. I said we'd see who is braver.

LITTLE CROW. The others with you, they decided to be brave too?

MEDICINE BOTTLE. We all went after them. *(Proudly displaying five newly-taken scalps.)* We killed three men and two women. *(The rattle stops as the SPIRIT GUIDE "takes" five "shots" created by five strikes of the drum. Silence. It's even worse than LITTLE CROW expected.)*

LITTLE CROW. And two women?

MEDICINE BOTTLE. Then we took their wagon and drove back to camp to tell what we had done. *(LITTLE CROW looks at them, utterly horrified. It's a moment before he can speak.)*

LITTLE CROW. It must be a very big wagon to carry all the punishment, suffering, death you've brought back to the Santee.

SHAKOPEE. It is a question of manhood.

LITTLE CROW. So you killed two women? My congratulations. But why tell your heroic exploits to me? Go talk to Traveling Hail.

SHAKOPEE. You're our chief, we need your experience. *(LITTLE CROW cannot suppress a grim ironic laugh.)*

LITTLE CROW. It's almost dawn. We should start appreciat-
ing every new dawn we see.

SHAKOPEE. Instead of waiting for the soldiers to come kill
us, let's strike first!

MEDICINE BOTTLE. Now! While they're fighting among
themselves to the south.

LITTLE CROW. No.

SHAKOPEE. With women killed, they'll take a dreadful vengeance.

LITTLE CROW. You are right.

SHAKOPEE. We have no choice.

LITTLE CROW. We do. We can accept their vengeance.

SHAKOPEE *(stunned)*. In place of fighting?

LITTLE CROW. In place of *extermination.*

MEDICINE BOTTLE *(the VOICE we've heard before, but
now a direct taunt). Kangi' ci' k'ala* is a coward! *(At this
challenge, the SPIRIT GUIDE sounds the rattle and rushes
frantically around LITTLE CROW.)* COWARD! *(MEDI-
CINE BOTTLE produces a knife for the "to-the-death"
fight that must follow. The rattle stops.)*

LITTLE CROW. This terrible word...coward. Is this word
worth the lives of all the young men who are going to die
for it? *(The rattle stops.) Is it? (MEDICINE BOTTLE and
SHAKOPEE are confused that LITTLE CROW has not answered the challenge.)* You are like little dogs in the Hot
Moon when they run mad and snap at their shadows. Open
your eyes and try to see. The white men are like the snow
when the sky is a blizzard. You may kill one-two-ten; yes,
as many as the leaves in the forest, and their brothers will
not miss them. Kill one-two-ten, and ten times ten will
come to kill you. Count your fingers all day long and white
men with guns will come faster than you can count.

SHAKOPEE. If we fight bravely...

LITTLE CROW. Talk bravery into the mouth of a cannon! You're fools.

SHAKOPEE. What should we do?

LITTLE CROW *(rattle sounds. Considers for a moment. There are no options).* There is only one thing you can do. Go, string your bows, make arrows, prepare for war...*(His voice chokes off.)*

SHAKOPEE. What will you do? *(Rattle out. The SPIRIT GUIDE freezes.)*

LITTLE CROW. *Kangi' ci' k'ala* is also a fool. *Kangi' ci' k'ala* will die with you. *(LITTLE CROW takes off Hoksila's coat and hands it to WOWINAPA. The "HUNT-ERS" break into war whoops and exit. Quietly, as from a great distance, war drums begin. LITTLE CROW crosses to remove his war bonnet from its display pole. The SPIRIT GUIDE thrusts his rattle from behind the pole and sends a furious warning. LITTLE CROW hesitates and then deliberately ignoring the warning, seizes his war bonnet.)*

WOWINAPA. Father...I'm coming with you.

LITTLE CROW *(sharply).* No. You will stay here...to get messages...*(LITTLE CROW puts on his war-bonnet.)*

WOWINAPA. Father...*(LITTLE CROW gestures for WOWINAPA to go; the boy exits with the display pole and Hoksila's coat.)*

SCENE 4D
Outside Fort Ridgely, Minnesota, August 18, 1862

(LITTLE CROW pulls the Santee staff from the ground. The drums roar; the SANTEE WAR PARTY charges into the circle and gathers around LITTLE CROW.)

LITTLE CROW. The attack has to be immediate, before they get word. Isolate soldiers in the fort; break into the ware-houses, take our food. *(War cries erupt and the WAR-RIORS explode into a war dance. When the frenzy of the dance nears its peak, LITTLE CROW signals and the WAR PARTY charges U and disappears over the ridge. The sound of the drums is shattered by a U.S. Army bugle sounding the alarm. Gunfire erupts and sounds of an ex-tended battle rage from the musicians. In the center of the circle, the SPIRIT GUIDE quietly prepares the space for death by offering burning sage to each of the four direc-tions. A lull in the battle allows MEDICINE BOTTLE and SHAKOPEE to desert over the ridge. LITTLE CROW fol-lows with the broken and charred Santee staff. He calls to the DESERTERS.)* Where are you going? We need your help.

SHAKOPEE. What can we do against a stone fort? This makes no sense. The smart thing is to raid the settlers...

LITTLE CROW. ...to kill farmers and their women? Santee braves make war on soldiers...*(A flurry of gunfire pulls LITTLE CROW's attention.)* Get back to your brothers. Now.

(LITTLE CROW disappears over the ridge as he moves back to his warriors. MEDICINE BOTTLE and SHAKOPEE ignore the order and race away; they are in-tercepted by WOWINAPA, entering.)

WOWINAPA. Where are the others? *(There is no answer.)* What are you doing here?

MEDICINE BOTTLE. Starting north; for Canada.

WOWINAPA. Do you want the *word* for what you are?

MEDICINE BOTTLE *(again, he shows his knife)*. Say that word and I'll kill you.

SHAKOPEE. Let's go! *(MEDICINE BOTTLE and SHAKOPEE run off.)*

BLACK ELK. Little Crow fought the great cannons, burned the fort and collected the food. The first killed was the government agent who told them, "If you're hungry, eat grass."

THE RELATIVE WHO PLAYS WOWINAPA *(to HOKSILA)*. Someone stuffed *his* mouth with grass.

BLACK ELK. Little Crow won a great battle; but there was no victory.

(LONG TRADER SIBLEY enters wearing a sword.)

WOWINAPA *(to BLACK ELK)*. Where is my father?

BLACK ELK. He goes west to warn the prairie Sioux. Go with him. Go, carry his bundles. *(WOWINAPA runs off L.)*

THE RELATIVE WHO PLAYS SIBLEY *(after WOWINAPA)*. And stay out of Minnesota!

SIBLEY *(to BLACK ELK)*. The Santee are holding white women hostage, trying to use white women for bargaining.

HOKSILA. What else can they use? You have all the cannons. *(Startled by this interruption, BLACK ELK and the RELATIVE playing SIBLEY turn to stare at the boy. HOKSILA retreats; SIBLEY continues.)*

SIBLEY. Release our women.

BLACK ELK. Your women are safe. They are in the custody of Santee who never joined the fighting; Santee anxious to exchange your women—unharmed—for the protection of your gratitude.

SCENE 4E
South Bend, Minnesota, December 26, 1862

THE RELATIVE WHO PLAYS SIBLEY *(to "the children").*
The moment we recovered the women, I rounded up every
male Santee still in Minnesota. *(On a muffled drum, A MU-*
SICIAN begins the slow cadence of the march to the scaf-
fold.) Three hundred and three were sentenced to the gallows. It was to be the greatest mass hanging in our history!
Then President Lincoln assigned hair-splitting, Indian-lov-
ing lawyers to review the convictions, which they "re-
viewed" down to just thirty-nine.

(The CONDEMNED PRISONERS enter UL, march up the
steps and stand evenly spaced across the front level of the
ridge. They wear black hoods and their hands are locked
behind their backs. They call to each other, "Hapan,"
"Traveling Hail," "Big Eagle," "Wabasha." The military
drum begins a roll. HOKSILA gets to his feet. He is very
agitated.)

SIBLEY. Look at them, trying to get their hands free; not the
slightest sign of human dignity. *(SIBLEY draws his sword*
and raises it above his head.) Let them pay for their
crimes, NOW! *(HOKSILA rushes into the center of the*
hoop.)

HOKSILA. No! *(SIBLEY cuts the air with his sword to signal*
the hangman. There is the sudden sound of the gallows
drop and complete silence. The heads of the condemned
have all snapped to the side. HOKSILA, in the center of the
hoop, turns away from the image of the hanged men and
stands trembling. BLACK ELK moves to him and speaks
quietly.)

BLACK ELK. They were trying to get their hands free to grasp another's hand. They were calling to their brothers to say, "I am with you! I am here." To say, "at this moment we are together. Together!" *(HOKSILA will not look at his grandfather. The boy walks away. BLACK ELK signals for the story to continue.)*

SIBLEY. We've never seen a finer military display in the state. *(SIBLEY sheathes his sword and exits. BLACK ELK signals for the SPIRIT GUIDE UC.)*

Hutchinson, Minnesota, July 3, 1863

(The SPIRIT GUIDE sounds his rattle as WOWINAPA and LITTLE CROW crawl out behind him. Little Crow's warbonnet is gone; the Santee staff is even more destroyed than when we last saw it; both men are dirty, ragged, and hungry.)

LITTLE CROW. We must go back. We must find any Santee still alive and bring them west. *(The SPIRIT GUIDE sounds a sustained rattle.)*

BLACK ELK. They reached the land where the big woods begin during the Moon of the Red Blooming Lilies. They did not know that all the remaining Santee had been driven out of Minnesota. *(A second rattle joins the first.)* They did not know the State of Minnesota was paying a scalp bounty of twenty-five dollars. *(A third rattle joins the other two.)* They did not know they were sighted by a farmer and his son as they came on a berry patch. *(A fourth rattle joins the other three.)*

LITTLE CROW. Raspberries! *(A single rifle shot cracks and LITTLE CROW falls. The rattles cease.)*

WOWINAPA. Father...

LITTLE CROW. Go! Get away!

WOWINAPA. No! I will not...

LITTLE CROW. They will kill you, too. Quickly! Quickly! You *must go! (He dies in his son's arms. "The other's still alive. Get him." are shouted from off-stage, followed by more shots. WOWINAPA hesitates before he runs.)*

WOWINAPA *(to himself). Kangi' ci' k'ala* was not a coward...*(To his father.) Kangi' ci' k'ala* was not a coward! *(To the world.) Kangi' ci' k'ala* was not a coward...*(As the flute begins to cry, WOWINAPA exits. The SPIRIT GUIDE lifts LITTLE CROW's body and carries it off R.)*

BLACK ELK *(to HOKSILA).* All that was left of the Santee in Minnesota were the skull and scalp of Little Crow preserved by the state historical society and put on exhibition in St. Paul.

(Music out. BLACK ELK crosses and picks up the remains of the Santee staff. The HANGED MEN remove their hoods and, as RELATIVES, exit UC. A RELATIVE enters and moves into the winter-telling circle. Before he can spin his wind-whistle, HOKSILA interrupts.)

HOKSILA *(tense, angry, and quick to blame).* Why didn't you stop them?

BLACK ELK. What?

HOKSILA. Why didn't you stop them from coming into our lands?

BLACK ELK *(avoids the question).* How could we know they were coming to kill our mothers and our children and us, and take everything for themselves?

HOKSILA. You could have stopped them.

BLACK ELK. How?

HOKSILA. By joining forces. All the tribes...together...had more warriors than they had soldiers.

BLACK ELK. But we were not together. Each one still thought himself an Arapaho, or Kiowa, or Crow, or some tribe of the Sioux—the Yankton, Brule, Blackfoot, Oglala, Hunkpapa...It will take much more to bring us together; to make us fight as one people...and the bluecoat soldiers provide "much more." They send a message screaming across the Colorado prairie no one can mistake. *(On BLACK ELK's signal, the RELATIVE begins to twirl a wind-whistle and a flurry of gunfire cuts through the howling wind.)*

SCENE 5A
A Cheyenne Camp near Smoky Hill, Colorado Territory
September 12, 1864

(An elder RELATIVE dressed as the PEACE CHIEF of the Southern Cheyenne rushes into the winter-telling circle. The CHIEF is very concerned; the gunfire means trouble for his people.)

THE CHEYENNE CHIEF. But why the Cheyenne? Why attack the Cheyenne? *(Wind-whistles out.)*

BLACK ELK. The white settlers have to pass through Cheyenne territory on the way to Pike's Peak in their rush for gold. Besides, the Cheyenne are so trusting, such an easy target.

(The CHIEF wears the classic Cheyenne eagle feather bonnet, an elaborately painted buckskin shirt trimmed with beads, breechclout and leggings; he plants the staff of the

Cheyenne nation inside the winter-telling circle. A RELA-
TIVE dressed as a CHEYENNE WOMAN joins the CHIEF.
She carries a very long "medicine bag.")

THE RELATIVE WHO PLAYS THE CHEYENNE CHIEF
(to "the children"). I am Black Kettle, Chief of the Southern Cheyenne. We know what happened to the Santee, so
we try every way to avoid the slightest provocation! We
are especially careful to keep the young men busy all the
time and out of trouble. If trouble comes anyway, we can
depend on two things to protect us. *(BLACK KETTLE pulls*
an American flag and three pieces óf a flag staff from the
"medicine bag" and begins to assemble it.) A soldier chief
gave us this magical flag. As long as we display it, no
soldier will ever fire on us. And we depend on a white
man—a soldier, my friend, Tall Chief Wynkoop.

THE RELATIVE WHO PLAYS THE CHEYENNE WOMAN.
The Cheyenne also depend on my husband. *(BLACK KET-*
TLE plants the flag next to the Cheyenne staff as THE
CHEYENNE WOMAN speaks to "the children.") I am
known as Yellow Woman; my blood is pure Cheyenne. My
husband, however, is white. The name of my husband is
"Little White Man," but he is also called, "William Bent."
A man of importance. There are three sons; all with un-
usual names, "Robert, George and Charles."

BLACK KETTLE. Where is Little White Man?

(TWO RELATIVES dressed as WASICHUS and a RELA-
TIVE dressed as a CHEYENNE CHIEF enter. They, too,
have heard the gunfire. One of the Wasichus is WILLIAM
BENT, a prosperous middle-aged fur trader; the other is
EDWARD WYNKOOP, a major in the U.S. Cavalry.)

YELLOW WOMAN. ...just returned from Fort Lyon with Major Wynkoop.

WILLIAM BENT. Is there trouble?

BLACK KETTLE (concerned about the implications). Lean Bear. Some soldiers were approaching; he rode out to greet them. They opened fire without warning; they shot Lean Bear out of his horse.

WYNKOOP. Colonel Chivington gave new orders for his soldiers to kill Cheyenne wherever found.

WILLIAM BENT. How can he go on the warpath? The man's an ordained minister! Madness!

BLACK KETTLE. Tall Chief Wynkoop, we must have peace.

WYNKOOP. I know. I don't understand what...(WYNKOOP and BLACK KETTLE and the other CHEYENNE CHIEF talk quietly. WILLIAM BENT crosses to YELLOW WOMAN.)

YELLOW WOMAN. This talk of peace does not appeal to strong young braves.

WILLIAM BENT. Yellow Woman, hear me, the strong young braves must stay very quiet. Where are our sons?

YELLOW WOMAN. Hunting on the Smoky Hill.

WILLIAM BENT. Good. I hope they stay there; they'll be much safer. You must go back to the ranch; avoid all white men...

YELLOW WOMAN (touching his face with affection). That is not entirely possible. (They share a laugh; YELLOW WOMAN exits. The CHEYENNE CHIEF exits as BLACK KETTLE and WYNKOOP cross to WILLIAM BENT.)

WYNKOOP. We have a plan.

BLACK KETTLE. Tall Chief Wynkoop wants me to talk with Colonel Chivington.

WYNKOOP. In Chivington's office in Denver. And it can't wait; we must start now.

(The CHEYENNE CHIEF re-enters followed by another CHIEF.)

BLACK KETTLE. I will bring the flag. We need the flag. *(BLACK KETTLE picks up the flag; the CHEYENNE CHIEF picks up the Cheyenne staff. The other CHIEF joins behind them.)*

WYNKOOP. We'll do a parade through Denver; then even the governor will know the Cheyenne's intentions. Chivington won't be able to ignore that. Forward march.

SCENE 5B
Denver, Colorado Territory, September 28, 1864

(The RELATIVE who will play the CROSSOVER SPIRIT appears on the ridge with open arms. She is dressed in white; her long black hair is worn in two braids. Her face and hands are painted white. Her palms are painted bright red. She has sprigs of sage hanging from each wrist. The MUSICIANS begin to sing the "Cheyenne March Song" to the accompaniment of hand drums. WYNKOOP and BENT complete the "parade." The PARADE moves sun-wise around the hoop in a choreographed procession through the streets of Denver. BLACK KETTLE dances and smiles as he waves his flag and calls, "Peace...peace." The other CHEYENNE are singing and dancing; BENT is self-conscious and uncomfortable; WYNKOOP, laughing, waves to the startled crowds. As the PARADE circles the outside of the hoop, the RELATIVES who will play COLONEL CHIVINGTON and LIEUTENANT CRAMER enter. CHIVINGTON carries a Bible; his long buckskin shirt is painted blue and gold with an enormous cross painted in

red in the center of the chest. When the PARADE stops,
BLACK KETTLE, WYNKOOP and BENT approach CHIV-
INGTON. The OFFICERS exchange salutes.)

WYNKOOP. Colonel Chivington.

CHIVINGTON *(speaking with a slight German accent).*
Major Wynkoop. Your command is Fort Lyon, Major!
What brings you to Denver?

WYNKOOP. The Cheyenne, sir, want to discover how to
make peace. *(BENT ushers BLACK KETTLE forward.)*
Colonel Chivington, this is Chief Black Kettle. He has
traveled many miles to speak with you. *(BLACK KETTLE*
offers to shake hands. CHIVINGTON does not respond.)

CHIVINGTON. What do you wish to say?

BLACK KETTLE. We have been traveling through a cloud.
The sky is dark ever since the fighting began. I want to tell
my people that from this day, the Cheyenne live in peace
with your people. I want to tell my people that I have taken
your hand. *(He again holds out a hand. CHIVINGTON*
smiles and clasps it.) Good. *(BLACK KETTLE crosses to*
WYNKOOP.) Thank you, my friend.

CHIVINGTON. Since you have such confidence in Major
Wynkoop, take your people to Fort Lyon where you can
live under his protection. You can make camp at Sand
Creek; there is good water, you will be safe there. As long
as you are camped at Sand Creek, you have our permission
to send your men west to hunt buffalo.

BLACK KETTLE. The herds to the west are large.

CHIVINGTON. Yes, your men can take plenty of meat;
enough for winter.

BLACK KETTLE. We will do as you say. *(On BLACK*
KETTLE's signal, a CHEYENNE CHIEF brings him the
American flag.) My people will winter at Sand Creek under

your protection and the protection of our magical flag. All we ask is to live in peace.

CHIVINGTON *(as BLACK KETTLE and the OTHERS exit).* Major Wynkoop, may I have a word with you?

WYNKOOP. Yes, sir.

CHIVINGTON. Why did you bring that filthy savage into Denver?

WYNKOOP. I...

CHIVINGTON. Do you really believe we can make peace with the Indians, Major?

WYNKOOP. Yes, sir.

CHIVINGTON. But it's not up to you, is it? *(Silence.)* Is it?

WYNKOOP. No, sir.

CHIVINGTON. Nor to me. I am not authorized to make peace with the redskins, Major. Our orders are, and I quote directly, "no peace until the Indians suffer," end quote. The savages must learn what it means to live in a Christian world. Besides, if we do make peace with the Indians, what will we do with the Third Colorado Regiment?

WYNKOOP. Fight the Confederates, sir.

CHIVINGTON. The Third Regiment was raised to kill Indians; it will kill Indians!

WYNKOOP. Any Indians? Unresisting Indians?

CHIVINGTON. I'm afraid you've lost your objectivity, Major. You won't be at Fort Lyon when Black Kettle arrives. Until further orders, you are confined to this post. You are dismissed, Major. *(WYNKOOP exits.)* Lieutenant Cramer, Colorado's Third Regiment is going to put down an Indian uprising. At Sand Creek.

CRAMER. Sir, the Cheyenne are moving to Sand Creek at our request; the United States has pledged safe passage for...

CHIVINGTON. Wynkoop had no authority...

CRAMER. You also pledged safety, sir.

CHIVINGTON. The Cheyenne are hostile; we now know where to intercept them, and...

CRAMER *(passion breaks through the training)*. We cannot attack a peaceful Cheyenne camp.

CHIVINGTON. They are hostiles.

CRAMER. If we attack, I say we dishonor this uniform.

CHIVINGTON. And I say any man who sympathizes with naked heathens is damned. Our orders are to kill Indians, Lieutenant. It is right and honorable to use any means under God's heaven to kill Indians!

CRAMER. Any means under God's heaven!? I don't understand that remark, sir.

CHIVINGTON. Ride with the regiment or report to the guard house under arrest. *(TWO RELATIVES begin to spin windwhistles. CHIVINGTON exits R; CRAMER exits L.)*

SCENE 5C
Sand Creek, Colorado Territory, November 29, 1864

(As the sound of a low wind moans quietly, the CROSS-OVER SPIRIT leads TWO CHEYENNE WARRIORS into the circle where they plant the Cheyenne staff and Black Kettle's American flag. The RELATIVE who plays YELLOW WOMAN follows.)

THE RELATIVE WHO PLAYS YELLOW WOMAN *(factually to "the children")*. All three of my sons would see what happened at Sand Creek.

(There's a distant sound of horses' hooves made by the drummers. The RELATIVE who will play the GRAND-

MOTHER enters. The GRANDMOTHER is seeking the source of the sound.)

THE RELATIVE WHO PLAYS YELLOW WOMAN. The foolish Cheyenne were so confident they had no sentries. Just before sunrise...

THE CHEYENNE GRANDMOTHER. Buffalo. Lots of buffalo coming into camp. *(Strains to see better.)* No, it's the pony herd; they've been frightened. *(Now with growing concern.)* Men on horses. *(Suddenly realizing.)* Soldiers! *(She screams the warning.)* Soldiers! Soldiers! *(The rest of the RELATIVES rush into the hoop as CHEYENNE—a GRANDFATHER; a MOTHER carrying a LITTLE GIRL; a LAME ELDER walking with a crutch; and a TEEN-AGED BOY. The drumming of the hooves is now very loud.)*

(BLACK KETTLE enters with his son, plucks his American flag from the ground and runs to the raised level.)

BLACK KETTLE. Come this way, up by the flag. Do not be afraid, the soldiers will not hurt you; but you must come here by the flag! You will be safe up here. Hurry! *(Some of the wary CHEYENNE move to the platform and huddle together under the flag, but FOUR CHEYENNE WARRIORS stay center staring at the approaching soldiers. BLACK KETTLE calls to them.)* Do not fight! Do not provoke the soldiers! Listen to me, the flag is your protection! Trust me! *(The WARRIORS obey and begin to move to BLACK KETTLE.)* No soldier will ever fire on the flag...*(Rifle fire cracks through the sounds of the wind and the hooves; A LITTLE GIRL falls forward and her dead body rolls down the ridge. TWO WARRIORS fall dead off the back of the ridge. BLACK KETTLE waves the flag frantically.)* Soldiers! The flag! We were promised! *(Another volley answers him. The Cheyenne staff is struck by a bullet; it explodes and the top half topples to the ground. TWO WARRIORS pull BLACK KETTLE off the ridge. The MOTHER rushes to the body of the LITTLE GIRL but she and the remaining Cheyenne are cut down in the hail of bullets.)*

THE RELATIVE WHO PLAYS YELLOW WOMAN *(her voice is flat, hollow)*. I don't know if there was such a high wind blowing or if the screaming was only in my mind. Seven hundred soldiers attacked. There were only thirty-five braves to face them. The rest were away, as they had been sent, hunting buffalo. The soldiers had been drinking whiskey during the night ride which might explain why they shot so poorly, and why a few Cheyenne escaped, including my sons, and Black Kettle. We might have been more prepared for what was to happen if we had known what Colonel Chivington had been saying. He urged the killing of Indian children as well because "nits make lice." Nits make lice! *(More shots are heard above the wind. Her voice as before, beyond emotion.)* As soon as the firing began, the warriors put the families together trying to protect them. But there were so few young men and soon they had been killed. A few of the women ran out to let the soldiers see they were women; and they begged for mercy. *(A volley of gunfire sounds. The wind stops under the shots.)* Their bodies were mutilated in such a way—I cannot say the words. The remaining women tried to hide in a ravine. When they saw the soldiers coming, they were so terrified they tied a bit of white cloth on a stick. They sent a child to walk toward the soldiers waving the white flag. Can you measure the terror? The terror that would make women send a child, a child? *(Seeing it. Hushed. Asking for it not to happen.)* No...No...

(A single shot shatters the air. YELLOW WOMAN tries to scream, but there's no sound. A SOLDIER with a torch moves from R to L behind the ridge. The crackling of fire can be heard; then the sky turns to flames as Chivington's soldiers burn the village. WILLIAM BENT enters, moves past the bodies of the dead, and rushes to his wife.)

WILLIAM BENT. Yellow Woman, I'm here. Wife!

YELLOW WOMAN *(verging on insanity)*. They will not let us live! They want our farmland, our hunting land; we do not have enough to give them; they still want more! There is nothing left, but to fight.

WILLIAM BENT *(trying to hold her)*. Listen to me!

YELLOW WOMAN *(breaking from him)*. We have to fight... *(YELLOW WOMAN picks up the top part of the broken Cheyenne staff and holds it as a weapon.)*...fight all of them.

WILLIAM BENT *(tries to approach her)*. I'm your husband. *(She swings the staff as a weapon to keep him from her.)* I'm your husband.

YELLOW WOMAN. You are one of them!

WILLIAM BENT. No! Never!

YELLOW WOMAN. You are a white man. I am starting north with my sons. *(She crosses to the ridge.)*

WILLIAM BENT. They're my sons too! They have my blood too!

YELLOW WOMAN. We are no part of any white man. *(A scream.)* We are *Cheyenne! (War drums and a war chant begin. YELLOW WOMAN and WILLIAM BENT exit in opposite directions, silhouetted by the raging fires.)*

SCENE 5D
On Smoky Hill, Colorado Territory, December 30, 1864

(A CHEYENNE WOMAN enters UC. Her hair is cut off; her dress is bloody and torn. She has rubbed ashes on her face, arms and legs. She carries the bloody and burned body of a child to the center of the hoop.)

BLACK ELK. With Sand Creek, the soldiers achieved what no Indian statesman had been able to contrive in generations; they made us start uniting.

(She lifts the body over her head and howls to the four directions. As she cries out, the drums and the war chant ceases. Dressed for war, REPRESENTATIVES of the Cheyenne, Arapaho, Kiowa and Sioux Nations enter; ONE GROUP moves to each of the four directions. The CHEYENNE UL; the ARAPAHO DL; the KIOWA DR; and the SIOUX UR. They watch the WOMAN in silence.)

BLACK ELK. No more Cheyenne,
          Arapaho, Kiowa, Sioux!
          We are one People!
          The Indian People!
(The war drums begin again. The CHEYENNE WOMAN lowers the CHILD and moves DC where she sits.)
Grandfathers, Great Spirit, we rub earth on ourselves to show that we are nothing without you. There is nothing upon which we can depend except you. Give us strength to defend the helpless ones!
(To the four Nations.)
          The white man has taken our country,
          Killed the buffalo;

Killed our wives and children.

Now, no peace!

ALL. No peace!

BLACK ELK. A thunder being nation we are.

ALL. We have said it.

BLACK ELK. A thunder being nation we are.

ALL. We have said it.

We shall live

We shall live

We shall live

BLACK ELK. We raise the battle-ax until death!

(BLACK ELK raises a tomahawk to the sky. The DRUM-
MERS begin to sing—the "Sioux Scouting War Song.")

MUSICIANS.

Paha Najio Hey Natah Heyape
Paha Najio Hey Natah Heyape
Paha Najio Hey Natah Heyape
Paha Najio Hey Natah Heyape

Mila Hanska Ki Hey Natah Heyuwe
Paha Najio Hey Natah Heyuwe
Paha Najio Hey Natah Heyape

(The WARRIORS from the separate nations merge into one
group dancing the same war dance. The dance builds for
several moments.)

ALL. *Hoka Hey!*

BLACK OUT—END OF ACT ONE

ACT TWO

SCENE 1A
A Ceremonial Ground in the Black Hills, October 1931

(At curtain time the lights go out. In the darkness, scores of war drums pound and then abruptly stop. Silence.

A flute is heard. Lights reveal the RELATIVES sitting in the winter-telling circle. The MEN are in war paint. On the highest level, a HOODED FIGURE sits motionless, his face and body obscured by a buffalo robe. FOUR RELA-TIVES dressed as CHIEFS—Kiowa, Arapaho, Cheyenne, and Lakota stand, each in one of the four directions. Each CHIEF carries several hoops, held in both hands, arms raised to shoulder level—reaching toward but not touching, the hoops of the CHIEF on each side. BLACK ELK stands in the center with a single hoop.)

BLACK ELK. The hoop is our tradition. Even our camp is arranged in a circle, as is all nature—the circle of the prairie horizon, of the unbitten moon, of the flow of life from seed to flower to seed again. *(As DRUMMERS join the flute—with the "Hoop Dance Song," a RELATIVE moves to the center of the circle, receives the hoop from BLACK ELK, and begins to dance. Each CHIEF lowers his hoops.)* The Cheyenne! *(The CHEYENNE CHIEF speaks in the Cheyenne language.)*

CHEYENNE CHIEF. *Tse tse-tas Eesh Honneh; Tse tse-tas Ekhonoaeh. (The DANCER takes the hoops from the*

64

CHIEF *and begins to move them around and over his body in a classic hoop dance.)*

BLACK ELK. The Arapaho! *(The ARAPAHO CHIEF speaks in the Arapaho language as the DANCER takes the hoops from him:)*

ARAPAHO CHIEF. *Heen Tooni' Henii se' nouni'.*

BLACK ELK. The Kiowa! *(The KIOWA CHIEF speaks in the Kiowa language as the DANCER takes the hoops from him:)*

KIOWA CHIEF. *Gwawyku De uh.*

BLACK ELK. The Sioux! *(The LAKOTA CHIEF speaks in the Lakota language as the dancer takes the hoops from him:)*

SIOUX CHIEF. *Lakota hepi; Lakota wanayolo. (The DANCER commits all of the hoops to create a series of images. At the finish, he steps out of his hoops and we discover they have been formed into a globe. He holds the globe aloft triumphantly. Music ends.)*

BLACK ELK. The many hoops of our Indian nations to-gether! *(Cheers and beating of drums; the WOMEN send the tremolo. The WARRIORS send battle cries.)* Our battle cry means, "It is a good day to die." Then we shout, "*Hoka hey,*"..."I am ready."

ALL. *Hoka hey! (TWO RELATIVES begin to spin wind-whis-tles.)*

BLACK ELK. The blizzard of whites is blowing toward the Black Hills, the sacred land of the Lakota Sioux; but when they invade, Chief Red Cloud mounts such a powerful counterattack, Washington decides negotiations might be more profitable. *(Wind-whistles out; the TWO RELATIVES exit.)*

SCENE 1B
Fort Laramie, Wyoming Territory, June 13, 1866

(The RELATIVE who will play RED CLOUD enters with the magnificent staff of the Lakota nation. He wears a single eagle feather in his long hair and a bone breastplate over his war shirt.)

BLACK ELK. Chief Red Cloud is a great warrior, a statesman of great skill, the most powerful chief of the Sioux Nation. *(RED CLOUD lifts the Lakota staff to each of the four directions.)* Since he has stopped the invasion, Red Cloud hopes this may prove an unusual negotiation; one in which there is something for the Indian. The prayers of Red Cloud are for what the Indian wants most from the government; something so rare we can only pray for it.

RED CLOUD. We pray that what is spoken here be the truth.

(Military and Native drums sound. The RELATIVE who will play COMMISSIONER TAYLOR enters UL. If he had not entered government service, TAYLOR would have become a used car salesman. He carries a star-spangled lap desk painted red, white and blue. The COMMISSIONER is accompanied by SOLDIER-AIDES, one carrying the Stars and Stripes, another carrying the territorial flag of Wyoming, and two others who place a small campaign table and chair inside the winter-telling circle and exit. The flags are placed behind and to each side of the chair in the classic positions. TAYLOR sits, takes papers from his lap desk and arranges them on the table. At the same time an ARAPAHO CHIEF, a KIOWA CHIEF and a CHEYENNE CHIEF enter UR and cross to flank RED CLOUD. Each carries the staff of his nation. Indian drums and songs

match and mix with the military drums. The military and native drums merge into a sonorous roll, rise to an honor beat, and fall silent. The ceremonial arrivals have been completed.)

TAYLOR *(rising and speaking with great charm in the accent of a senator from the deep south).* Chief Red Cloud, my name is Ezra Booth Taylor. I am president of the Treaty Commission. The United States government is anxious to reach an agreement to open the Bozeman Road through your territory. *(A murmur moves through RED CLOUD's party.)* We only need a little bit of land.

RED CLOUD. How little?

TAYLOR. Only as much as a wagon would take between the wheels.

RED CLOUD. There are white people all around us. They come like a river dirty with lies and greed. We have but a small spot of land left. The Great Spirit tells us to keep it.

TAYLOR *(with the demonstrated patience of one used to dealing with children).* But, there's been a discovery in Montana, the yellow metal. We expect heavy travel.

RED CLOUD. Such travel would violate our treaty.

TAYLOR. Yes. The old treaty. We are here to make a new treaty.

RED CLOUD. We have a signed treaty. If your soldiers come into our country, we'll fight them.

TAYLOR. Why this talk of fighting?

(As TAYLOR continues, FOUR RELATIVES enter. One will play COLONEL HENRY B. CARRINGTON; another, a LAKOTA MESSENGER. CARRINGTON who is escorted by TWO SOLDIERS moves to a position behind TAYLOR. The

MESSENGER crosses the ridge, jumps to the floor and whispers in RED CLOUD's ear.)

TAYLOR. Why not talk of our friendship for our red brothers, of the train we have loaded ready to bring presents? I have a manifest of these presents which I would like to read to you in detail. The generosity of the Great Father, his consideration for your welfare, bales of fine blankets, tins of prime tobacco...

RED CLOUD. This officer was met some distance from here and asked where he and his men were going.

TAYLOR *(seeing CARRINGTON for the first time).* Colonel Carrington! You're early, Colonel.

CARRINGTON *(speaks with a British accent).* We made good time.

TAYLOR. Our negotiations are...We were not expecting you until...

CARRINGTON. To avoid any chance of trouble, I halted my regiment four miles east of the post.

RED CLOUD. That is very tactful. And from there, Colonel?

CARRINGTON. What?

RED CLOUD. You are now less than *two* miles east of this post and less than one mile from the border between our two nations. Do you intend to turn north into our territory?

CARRINGTON. You have no right to interrogate an officer of the...

TAYLOR. Colonel Carrington.

RED CLOUD. We have made special prayers; prayers that you tell us the truth!

TAYLOR *(a considered pause. Drops his cordial mask).* The truth is that we are going to open the Bozeman Road.

RED CLOUD. Congratulations. For telling the truth.

TAYLOR. How dare you speak to me in this outrageous...

RED CLOUD *(interrupting with cool and controlled purpose)*. Why do you treat Indians like children?

TAYLOR. I represent the government of the United States...

RED CLOUD. Why do you pretend to negotiate for our country while preparing to take it with your soldiers?

TAYLOR. It is only a matter of a road, a few forts. Because of the seasonal requirements we...The Great Father sends presents!

RED CLOUD. While this soldier goes to steal our land before the Indians say yes or no. This earth is my mother. For what presents should I sell my mother?

TAYLOR. You don't speak for all Indians. *(RED CLOUD pulls his staff from the ground.)* Others would like to hear about the annuities, about the wealth of supplies...

RED CLOUD. Any Indian wishing to sell the home of The People stay here and negotiate. *(RED CLOUD turns abruptly and exits. With equal abruptness, he is followed by the other CHIEFS and all of the remaining PEOPLE.)*

TAYLOR. You haven't even heard the offer! *(But they are gone.)* Savages! Does he think we're going to leave valuable land as a camping ground for nomads! *(To CARRINGTON.)* In any case I don't expect he'll give you much trouble. *(CARRINGTON turns a slow stare to the civilian.)* How many wagons are you escorting?

CARRINGTON. Two hundred—enough tools and personnel to erect four new forts before the first snow.

TAYLOR *(as they exit)*. Move them north tomorrow morning. We are authorized to open the road and to use any measures to protect our citizens.

SCENE 1C

Near Fort Kearny, Wyoming Territory, July 16, 1866

(RED CLOUD enters followed by the THREE CHIEFS. They sit in a war council.)

HOKSILA. They break the treaty!

BLACK ELK. Again. We are at war. Again. A war we must win to survive.

RED CLOUD *(to the War Council).* One nation cannot fight them alone. The soldiers meet our arrows with cannons and rifles that shoot many times. We must join together...many warriors for each soldier.

KIOWA CHIEF. All our warriors together cannot open one of their forts. *(The other CHIEFS murmur in agreement. RED CLOUD has reached an impasse.)*

BLACK ELK. Then we discover the most formidable weapon ever created by the Indian people...

HOKSILA. Weapon? *(BLACK ELK points to the highest ledge where the HOODED FIGURE, enclosed by the wings of THE EAGLE SPIRIT, sits in prayer. The music of the flute and the Aleut drum—playing the "Crazy Horse Motif"—speaks to the other world.)*

BLACK ELK. He purifies himself in preparation for the battle. He seeks strength from the world of his vision. *(As the EAGLE SPIRIT releases him, smoke rises around the HOODED FIGURE. When he looks to the sky, his buffalo robe drops away revealing a YOUNG MAN clad only in a breechclout.)*

THE YOUNG MAN. The world men live in is only a shadow of the real world, which is the world of the spirit. In the real world, the world beside this one, everything floats and dances because it is made of the spirit and nothing is material. *(He rises.)* In the real world, I am on my horse and we dance through trees and rocks. *(He disappears. The EAGLE begins to dance slowly to the flute and drums.)*

BLACK ELK. He cares nothing for possessions, not even ponies. If game is scarce and The People are hungry, he will not eat. He is usually so preoccupied he does not see or hear others. Yet within his young body there is something that spreads around him in battle like wind blowing fire through grass. When he leaves his vision quest, he brings us what we need much more than courage—a genius for military tactics. *(Music out. The EAGLE SPIRIT freezes in tableau.)* His name is Crazy Horse.

(The EAGLE SPIRIT sends the cry of an eagle. CRAZY HORSE enters and stands apart from the war council. He has added leggings to the breechclout; his upper body is painted with blue spots; a red lightning bolt slashes across one side of his face.)

RED CLOUD. The bluecoats have retreated to their forts. We cannot get inside to kill them.

CRAZY HORSE. Then we must bring them out.

RED CLOUD. Bring them out? How?

CRAZY HORSE. Decoys.

KIOWA CHIEF. Decoys! Against cannons?

CRAZY HORSE. If the soldiers see one of us make an insulting gesture, they get hot, make mistakes. We used this weakness to kill a lieutenant, a sergeant and several others.

RED CLOUD. Tell us.

CRAZY HORSE. I dismounted, showed myself in front of some young cavalry officers; they left the fort, came charging after me. As soon as I had them strung out behind, my men hit them from the side.

KIOWA CHIEF. A useful skirmish.

CRAZY HORSE *(pressing his point)*. The same tactic could entice a large number of troops into a useful *battle! (The KIOWA CHIEF begins to protest as the ARAPAHO CHIEF also begins to speak.)*

RED CLOUD *(to the CHIEFS)*. Wait! He has discovered this is so. *(Considering.)* A useful battle...*(To the OTHER CHIEFS.)* If you will join with us, we will try it. *(The CHEYENNE and ARAPAHO CHIEFS nod in assent. The KIOWA CHIEF does not agree.)* This will require special organization. *(RED CLOUD and the CHIEFS exit R.)*

SCENE 1D
Near Fort Kearny, Wyoming Territory, December 12, 1866

(The drums begin. From the center of the circle, CRAZY HORSE sends prayers; on the ridge, the movements of the EAGLE SPIRIT carry his prayers to the sky.)

BLACK ELK. The warriors prepare a few miles from Fort Kearny. Red Cloud assembles an unusual war party of Cheyenne, Arapaho and Sioux—at last, three nations united as one people.

(RED CLOUD appears on the bluff with the Lakota staff.)

BLACK ELK. When Red Cloud has our main party in position, Crazy Horse and his decoys make the first move.

CRAZY HORSE *(whispers)*. Hoka Hey. *(The drums crescendo. In a choreographed sequence, CRAZY HORSE crawls to the D side of the hoop where he leaps to his feet, waves a red blanket and sends the cry of an eagle. He then*

*faces "the fort." There is the heavy thump of a howitzer
firing; CRAZY HORSE appears terrified; he runs this way
and that as though confused. He stops, again faces "the
fort," and lifts the front of his breechclout in an insulting
gesture. This is answered with the classic bugle call for a
U.S. Army cavalry charge followed by a thundering of
hooves and the confident shouts of men who know they
have their enemy on the run. CRAZY HORSE races UC,
leaps onto the ridge, and turns to watch with clinical interest.)*

RED CLOUD *(also clinical).* They committed a major force,
almost a hundred men.

CRAZY HORSE. Because an Indian is impudent! I will keep
them coming. *(CRAZY HORSE disappears UR; the EAGLE
DANCER exits.)*

BLACK ELK. The force from the fort is commanded by Cap-
tain Fetterman who is under explicit orders from Colonel
Carrington not to pursue beyond Lodge Trail Ridge. But
Crazy Horse rides along that ridge!

(CRAZY HORSE reappears UL.)

CRAZY HORSE. Cowards. COWARDS!

*(With a thunder of hooves, the cavalry charges into view
with flags flying; CRAZY HORSE races off the ridge into
the valley created by the circle. The SOLDIERS pursue him
down from "the ridge." RED CLOUD raises his lance and
is answered by a burst of war cries topped with gunfire.
The SOLDIERS fall dead, arrows sticking from their bodies in various angles. Silence. HOKSILA breaks into the
circle with a shout. He leaps over the bodies as he counts
coups and sings, "One little, two little, three little whities;
four little, five little..." The MUSICIANS and the RELA-*

TIVE who plays RED CLOUD "drop character" to laugh at the boy.)

BLACK ELK. Captain Fetterman, who foolishly got himself and all his men killed, had a fort named in his honor. Colonel Carrington, whose sensible orders were disobeyed, was recalled from command.

HOKSILA. We may win this war, yet. *(BLACK ELK laughs—this time joined by the RELATIVES who are playing dead soldiers.)*

Near Fort Laramie, Wyoming Territory, Spring 1868

(The RELATIVES who play COMMISSIONER TAYLOR and GENERAL SHERMAN enter and are startled by the spectacle that greets them. BLACK ELK gestures for the "dead" to resume their prone positions. TAYLOR eyes the dead soldiers and then petulantly stomps his foot.)

TAYLOR. We want to make a new treaty.

RED CLOUD. No.

TAYLOR. But why not?

RED CLOUD. I will not talk peace until your soldiers leave my country.

GENERAL SHERMAN *(calls up to the bluff where RED CLOUD stands with the Lakota staff. He speaks with a Yankee accent)*. Chief Red Cloud...

BLACK ELK *(identifies the GENERAL for HOKSILA)*. Great Warrior General Sherman. General William Tecumseh Sherman.

GENERAL SHERMAN. If, on examination, we find that the Bozeman Road hurts you, we will give it up.

RED CLOUD. If that were true...

TAYLOR. Or pay for it. We sent a supply of tobacco...

RED CLOUD *(from above)*. And I will smoke it. As soon as the soldiers leave my country.

GENERAL SHERMAN *(to TAYLOR)*. This is an embarrassment and a humiliation, but I don't see alternatives.

TAYLOR *(under)*. The only way to deal with these...

GENERAL SHERMAN. The only way is to end it. It's too expensive. The Indian Wars are costing us millions. What do we have to show for it? A handful of dead Indians. The War Department wants an immediate treaty. Tell Red Cloud...

RED CLOUD *(calling down to them)*. When we see the soldiers moving south and the forts abandoned, I will come down to talk about a new treaty. *(RED CLOUD exits.)*

SHERMAN *(swears under his breath; then makes the decision)*. Abandon the forts north of the Platte.

TAYLOR. Sir?

GENERAL SHERMAN. My special competence is military reality. Red Cloud has given us a beating. Abandon the forts! *(With this, SHERMAN exits leaving TAYLOR aghast. A bugle sounds "retreat"; the dead soldiers rise, form into ranks behind their flags, and march in retreat.)*

Fort C.F. Smith, Wyoming Territory, July 30, 1868

(As the DRUMMERS sing the "Chief's Song," RED CLOUD, CRAZY HORSE and three other CHIEFS, appear on the ridge with the staffs of the Sioux, Cheyenne, Kiowa and the Arapaho nations.)

MUSICIANS.
> *Oyate ki unsi malayapi ca*
> *Tegi giha oma waniyelo*
> *Wicas Ianca Ki Heya giyape*

RED CLOUD. Burn their forts.

(FOUR WARRIORS WITH TORCHES rise from behind the ridge and move into the winter-telling circle. They dance the burning of the forts to frenetic drums. The FIVE CHIEFS watch from above.)

Near Fort Laramie, Wyoming Territory, November 6, 1868

(As the TORCH-DANCERS exit, BLACK ELK unrolls a buffalo robe center. The FIVE CHIEFS move to the buffalo robe and plant the four staffs behind it. CRAZY HORSE stands beside the Sioux staff, the other CHIEFS by the Arapaho, Kiowa and Cheyenne staffs. RED CLOUD sits on the buffalo robe, waiting... TAYLOR enters behind a SOLDIER carrying a white flag. When TAYLOR sees the Indians, he stops, considers his options, and then reluctantly sits on the buffalo robe where he removes the treaty, pen and ink from his lap desk.)

RED CLOUD. What does <u>this</u> treaty say about the home of The People?

TAYLOR *(reads)*. No white person shall be permitted to settle upon or occupy any portion of the Black Hills, or, without the consent of the Indians, to pass through the same. *(RED CLOUD looks to the CHEYENNE CHIEF who nods; he looks to the KIOWA CHIEF who nods. He looks to the ARAPAHO CHIEF who nods.)*

RED CLOUD. Present the pen. Our peoples desire peace, and
I pledge my honor to maintain it. *(TAYLOR passes two
copies of the treaty to RED CLOUD and offers the pen.
RED CLOUD takes the pen and signs both copies.)*
BLACK ELK. I am angry with our chief, Red Cloud.
HOKSILA. Why?
BLACK ELK. From the moment he touched the pen to this
new treaty renouncing war, he never fought again.

*(RED CLOUD returns the treaty copies to TAYLOR who
signs both and returns one. RED CLOUD rises with his
copy and leads the procession of the FIVE CHIEFS up the
ridge and off. The MUSICIANS break into song—the
"Lakota Victory Song." From over the ridge, dancing and
singing LAKOTAS pour into the winter-telling circle. Some
are carrying baskets; some are carrying weapons.
HOKSILA lifts the buffalo robe and begins to spin in exultant celebration.)*

MUSICIANS and LAKOTAS.
Paha Najio Paha Najio
Paha Najio Paha Najio
Nake nòla
Ceya He Unke
BLACK ELK *(shouts down the demonstration).* No. No. *(He
pulls the buffalo robe from HOKSILA and throws it to the
ground. The music and dancing stop. There is a stunned
silence.)* Why do you celebrate this treaty? Do you really
believe the United States government will keep its prom-
ise? *(The celebrating LAKOTAS sit outside the hoop as
RELATIVES.)* Railroad tracks cut across our land, dividing
what is left of the buffalo herds. Hot-heads among the
Southern Cheyenne give the United States government its

excuse to break this new treaty. These young fools derail a train, break in, drink whiskey, then tie ends of cloth bolts they find in the baggage to their ponies' tails and ride across the prairie with these streamers flying behind them.

(A RELATIVE spins a wind-whistle and the RELATIVE who plays CUSTER enters on the ridge and stands looking down. His elaborate gold-fringed buckskin shirt is painted blue on top with vertical red and white stripes around the bottom. From under his hat cascades long auburn horse hair; a blue lightening bolt slashes across a cheek of its wearer telling us that CUSTER is played by the RELATIVE who plays CRAZY HORSE.)

BLACK ELK. The forces sent to deal with this "threat to civilization" include the glory-hunter George Armstrong Custer. At twenty-three, he became their youngest general. He led large forces in their Civil War. When he finished with the graycoats, his trail turned north to a collision with our youngest, Crazy Horse! They are almost exactly the same age; they each have a strangeness; they are both great leaders; but there is a difference—one of them is a savage!

SCENE 2
The Washita River, Oklahoma Territory
November 26, 1868

(BLACK KETTLE enters with the part of the Cheyenne staff that was carried away from Sand Creek by YELLOW WOMAN. It has been lashed to a new base, it has fared badly since we last saw it. BLACK KETTLE places the staff inside the hoop and moves to the center of the circle

where he begins to chant quietly to himself. He looks much older. He has not coped well with the betrayals at Sand Creek.)

BLACK ELK. The boys breaking into the train give Custer his excuse for massive retaliation. It does not matter that all he will find along the Washita River are the frightened Cheyenne, survivors of Sand Creek, trying to find safety with Black Kettle.

(CUSTER begins to circle BLACK KETTLE— moving counter-clockwise around the outside of the hoop.)

BLACK KETTLE. My mind is sometimes feeble...does not always produce order.

(A RELATIVE stands as the CHEYENNE GRAND-MOTHER and moves to BLACK KETTLE. As his anxiety rises, she soothes him with a lullaby sung by Lakota mothers to their babies.)

CHEYENNE GRANDMOTHER.
*Ink pata Na Wajin, Na Wa Sina Ci Cu Ze
Maya Miya Le Geya Ku Wa Na.*

BLACK KETTLE. Sometimes the nightmare of Sand Creek comes...it is so real...There is bad talk...Custer and his pony soldiers...this *is* real...not...my mind. *(A RELATIVE rises and crosses DR.)* The best hope...move our lodges south...But I am told we must stay by the Washita River! *(The RELATIVE begins to spin a wind-whistle creating the low moaning sounds heard at Sand Creek; a SECOND RELATIVE stands. CUSTER continues to circle.)* Something...runs loose...in my mind. Am I looking at the

Washita River...or am I seeing Sand Creek? *(The SEC-OND RELATIVE begins to spin a wind-whistle.)* I don't know if it is such a high wind blowing...or if the screaming is only in my mind. *(TWO MORE RELATIVES stand and begin to spin wind-whistles. On CUSTER's hand signal, "move forward at a gallop," the DRUMMERS begin the sound of horses' hooves. The GRANDMOTHER looks to the horizon.)*

THE GRANDMOTHER *(concerned, but not frightened)*. Buffalo. Lots of buffalo coming into camp. *(As before.)* No, it is the pony herd.

BLACK KETTLE. ...the nightmare again...

THE GRANDMOTHER *(frightened. Pointing)*. Men on horses coming from every direction. *(Now she realizes.)* Soldiers!

BLACK KETTLE *(shouts to her)*. Woman, calm yourself!

THE GRANDMOTHER. Pony soldiers! Soldiers are coming!

BLACK KETTLE. If soldiers were coming, we would hear the drumming of hooves!

THE GRANDMOTHER. We cannot hear them!

BLACK KETTLE. Because it's a dream.

THE GRANDMOTHER *(frantic)*. Because of the snow! *(CUSTER signals for the charge.)*

BLACK KETTLE. ...the snow...*(A bugle sounds the cavalry charge.)* Bugles! There were no bugles! *(Shots are being fired. BLACK KETTLE rejoins reality. He rushes to the Cheyenne staff and raises it as he shouts.)* We are under attack! Get mounted! Scatter! Escape! C-h-e-y-e-n-n-e-s! *(The RELATIVES watching the story leap to their feet and rush into the winter-telling circle as Cheyenne. Some carry baskets, some weapons. The RELATIVES spinning the wind-whistles become CHEYENNE WARRIORS. Hundreds of shots are fired. The choreographed massacre is very fast, very brutal, and when it is over, the stage is covered with carnage. The wind has stopped. CUSTER is gone.)*

(A tinkle of bone chimes sounds; the CROSSOVER SPIRIT appears on the ridge. She signs "heart; see; no more." HOKSILA moves down through the bodies and pulls the Cheyenne staff from BLACK KETTLE's dead hands.)

BLACK ELK. Custer's men killed one hundred and three Cheyenne. Eleven were warriors...*(HOKSILA crosses away from his grandfather and pushes the staff into the junk-pile. The sound of a military band playing the rousing "Garry Owen" cuts through the silence. Behind the ridge where the CROSSOVER WOMAN is exiting, Custer's hat and the tops of the Stars and Stripes and the 7th Cavalry battle flag can be seen passing from L to R.)*

SCENE 3A
Louisville, Kentucky, February, 1873

(The DEAD rise, reach into the baskets and transform into wasichu CUSTER SUPPORTERS—the MEN by putting on vests and derbies or top hats, and the WOMEN by adding bonnets, shawls and parasols. The washichu clothes are red, white, and blue. The CUSTER SUPPORTERS begin to dance an Irish jig on the graves of the massacred Cheyenne to the "Garry Owen." As the band music grows louder, the FLAG BEARERS reappear on top of the ridge and march the Stars and Stripes and the 7th Cavalry Battle Flag into position at the back of the level that will serve as a speakers' platform. The CUSTER SUPPORTERS begin to wave small American flags and chant "Custer! Custer!

*Custer!" The RELATIVE who will play the newspaperman,
JOHN FINERTY, enters with a large box camera on a tri-
pod which he delivers to the RELATIVE who will become
his PHOTOGRAPHER. FINERTY wears a derby and a
red, white, and blue plaid coat; enthusiastic and star-
struck, he speaks with an aggressive Irish brogue.
FINERTY crosses to the top of the "speaker's platform."
The PHOTOGRAPHER begins to set up his camera on the
ground below.* "Garry Owen" *ends.)*

FINERTY *(announcing to the crowd and displaying the head-
line of his paper; he speaks in a broad Irish accent).* My
name is John Finerty of the Chicago Times. I am proud to
introduce two great American generals, heroes of the Civil
War, heroes of the Indian Wars! General George Crook...
three-star General Crook...*(There is polite applause and
some cheering as the RELATIVE who will play CROOK
moves to the speaker's platform, touches the brim of his
hat and joins FINERTY at the side.)* And...*George Armstrong CUSTER!!*

*(Pandemonium breaks out as CUSTER moves onto the
platform.)*

CUSTER *(spotting the PHOTOGRAPHER ready to take his
picture, holds his gloved hand in the air and coos in a
slight Irish accent).* Hurrah for Custer's luck! *(He holds the
pose waiting for the flash. The CUSTER SUPPORTERS
gather under Custer's platform, in front of the camera, to
be included in the photograph.)*

FINERTY *(to CROOK).* Legend in our own time! Our next
president!

PHOTOGRAPHER. Ready, aim...(*The flash powder ignites and the crowd cheers. CUSTER quiets them.*)

CUSTER. I have pacified the plains; the Great Plains are secure! (*The crowd cheers wildly.*) The Savage has been taught a lesson he'll never forget. The Indian thought he could live anywhere he likes; his manner was getting lofty and independent. Not any more; I whipped the Indian into submission! (*More cheers.*)

A WHITE MAN. General Custer...sir. Not all Indians are hostile. Some are good people. (*There is annoyance in the crowd reaction, but CUSTER delighted with the cue that has been handed to him, waves for silence.*)

CUSTER. In the immortal words of General Sheridan, "The only good Indian is a dead Indian." (*Hoots, laughter and applause from the CROWD.*)

THE WHITE MAN. I never heard that.

CUSTER (*waves for silence*). From here I go north again, back to the Black Hills. And I have wonderful news. I can confirm all rumors about the Black Hills—from the grass roots down, *gold!* (*The CROWD goes wild.*) The prospectors will be protected; I'll see to it personally. I will take back the Black Hills, then...on to the Big Horn! (*Cheers and military music as the exultant CUSTER struts off followed by GENERAL CROOK and the FLAGS. The CROWD exits.*)

THE RELATIVE WHO PLAYS FINERTY (*to HOKSILA*). I have the assignment of my life! I'm to accompany the Big Horn expedition to cover...(*He reads FINERTY's prose from the newspaper.*) "the final destruction of the savage, the barbarous descendants of Cain presently occupying the magnificent territory from the Black Hills to the Big Horn." (*He gives the paper to HOKSILA.*) My wish is to go with Custer, who will attack from the north, but I'm assigned to General Crook who will march up simultaneously from the south in a sophisticated attack designed in the form of a great military nutcracker...*(FINERTY touches the fingers of each hand together and then closes his palms making the crunching motion of a nutcracker.)*

SCENE 3B
Near the Headwaters of the Rosebud River
Montana Territory, June 17, 1876

(Battle sounds are heard. CRAZY HORSE enters on the DR bluff, the EAGLE SPIRIT enters on the top level.)

FINERTY *(explaining the flurry of gunfire to HOKSILA as though the boy is one of CROOK's soldiers).* Our scouts found a Sioux village on the Rosebud River. We'll crash through there; then drive on to the Big Horn to join General Custer, and...

(RELATIVES who will play GENERAL CROOK and an AIDE rush on from L.)

FINERTY. General Crook, sir, what's the delay? *(CROOK glances at him and then back at the battle through a field glass.)* Sir, I assume the savages greatly outnumber us...

CROOK *(over his shoulder).* I don't think that's the problem.

FINERTY. ...but our weapons are superior. They *are* superior. What is the problem?

CROOK *(gestures toward CRAZY HORSE).* Him. *(With a mirror CRAZY HORSE flashes signals from the bluff to his WARRIORS below. FINERTY watches with astonishment.)*

FINERTY. Who is it?

CROOK *(as he swings his glass to the battlefield)*. My first thought, it has to be Robert E. Lee; but these tactics are a bit more innovative. *(To the AIDE.)* They're infiltrating down the ravine. We have to pull back...again. *(The AIDE hurries off.)*

FINERTY. What's his name?

CROOK. Crazy Horse.

FINERTY. A savage named *Crazy Horse* is causing difficulty for the United States Army? *(CROOK gives him a pained glance and turns back to the battle.)* Sir. General Crook, when will we break through and drive on to meet Custer?

CROOK. Go ask Crazy Horse. *(CROOK, shouting to his field commanders, crosses L to exit.)* Time to move.

FINERTY. Why can't you force these savages to respect the treaties?

CROOK *(pauses. A bitter laugh)*. The Indians didn't break this treaty. *(CROOK exits.)*

THE RELATIVE WHO PLAYS FINERTY *(turns to see HOKSILA staring at CRAZY HORSE)*. Why does he fight like this? He could sell this land for a great deal of money. *(HOKSILA starts to provide a flip "comeback" but freezes. He turns back to the RELATIVE who plays CRAZY HORSE.)*

THE RELATIVE WHO PLAYS CRAZY HORSE. One does not sell the earth upon which The People walk.

HOKSILA *(turns back to the RELATIVE who plays FINERTY)*. One does not sell the earth upon which The People walk.

THE RELATIVE WHO PLAYS FINERTY. Or do you?

FINERTY *(to HOKSILA)*. Are you coming with us? *(HOKSILA shakes his head. The RELATIVE takes FINERTY's newspaper from the boy, and exits L. HOKSILA turns to CRAZY HORSE.)*

CRAZY HORSE. When I am in the world of men and things, I watch soldiers—their soldiers, ours—and the ways of fighting. Then I dream myself into the real world, that world of the spirit, the world beside this world, and seek visions to protect The People. My vision tells me their soldiers will fight in the old way, but we must not fight in our old way. *(BLACK ELK signals the DRUMMERS who respond with the rolling sound of the sneak-up beat. CRAZY HORSE drops down from the top of the bluff and crosses to the center of the circle where he rallies a thousand warriors. HOKSILA moves with him.)* LAKOTAS! We will surprise General Crook by attacking his skirmish lines from the flanks. Break the big battle into many little battles. Find openings, get in among them, create confusion, frustration. Do not charge into massed firepower hoping to perform brave foolish deeds for the retelling. Do not stop to count coups or take scalps or capture horses. Do not get tired or hungry and decide to break off. We are Lakotas! We fight for our nation! *(CRAZY HORSE throws back his head and sends the cry of an eagle. The EAGLE SPIRIT sends back the cry, and the roar of battle cries and gunfire erupts from all sides. As the battle rages, CRAZY HORSE moves to the UC platform. From this perch, he watches until he sees something that causes his legs to sag under him. He drops to his knees and then turns and shouts.)* The bluecoats are moving south. In retreat. They are leaving the land of The People! *(The WOMEN send tremolos. Inside CRAZY HORSE's head, something begins to whisper to him.)* These soldiers are not alone. Custer! Where is he? *(He turns and barks orders to HOKSILA as though the boy was one of his warrior chiefs.)* Take a few warriors; show yourselves to Crook; start grass fires; shoot into his camp at night; keep him moving south. *(He moves to the top of*

the ridge where he calls again for the vision.) Where,
where is Custer? *(The EAGLE SPIRIT quivers its wings
and sends the cry of an eagle. The vision comes. CRAZY
HORSE whispers quietly.)* Little Big Horn. *Hoka Hey.
(CRAZY HORSE disappears behind the ridge. The EAGLE
SPIRIT disappears UR.)*

SCENE 4
On the Little Big Horn River, Montana Territory
June 25, 1876

*(The DRUMMERS set the rhythm for the choreographed
ritual of the Battle of Little Big Horn.)*

BLACK ELK. I was thirteen years old that day, swimming in
the Little Big Horn with other boys. There is no warning in
the beautiful sky; no warning that Custer's troops are moving south to crush us. *(The drums rise sharply with the
beat of hooves.)* I hear the cry going from camp to camp,
"They are coming! They are coming!" I hear our women
screaming! The sky fills with dust and thunder. *(The bugle
sounds. BLACK ELK speaks to HOKSILA from somewhere
between his memories and a total reliving of the battle. The
passion of the old man frightens HOKSILA.)* Then I see
him, riding along the ridge, The Wolf of Washita! He pulls
up for a moment, deciding where to attack. He sees terrified women running for cover, men trying to find their
brothers, catch their ponies. *(A new blast from the bugle.
Decisions have been made. The battle begins.)* The first
charge catches women and children in the open. Many are
killed. There is panic everywhere. Then a great cry goes
up: Crazy Horse is coming! Crazy Horse is coming!

C-R-A-Z-Y H-O-R-S-E! Custer tries to get to the river, but he is driven back to the high ridge. He is up there, the Wolf of Washita, Hard Backsides, Long Hair, Squaw Killer, George Armstrong Custer! Suddenly, all at once, like bees swarming out of a hive, like a hurricane! *(A battle cry.)* L-A-K-O-T-A-S! *There... never... was... a... better... day... to... die!*

(LAKOTA WARRIORS suddenly appear from behind the ridge.)

WARRIORS *(weapons aloft. A great shout)*. HOKA HEY! *(The sound of a huge explosion marks the clash of forces as a brilliant flash of light obliterates the landscape. When the eyes adjust, the WARRIORS and the battle sounds are gone. CRAZY HORSE stands alone in the center of the hoop with the dust and the smoke of the battle still around him. He holds the broken and charred staff of the Lakota nation. CRAZY HORSE is exhausted; HOKSILA, awe-struck, stands looking at him. A flute sings softly. HOKSILA approaches CRAZY HORSE.)*

HOKSILA. I am told a Santee killed Custer.

CRAZY HORSE. Yes.

HOKSILA. Someone else said it was White Bull of the Minneconjous.

CRAZY HORSE. Yes.

HOKSILA. I thought probably you killed him.

CRAZY HORSE. Yes.

THE RELATIVE WHO PLAYS CRAZY HORSE. You killed him too.

SCENE 5A
The Western Plains, Summer 1876-Spring 1877

BLACK ELK. Word reaches them July 4, 1876—their centennial celebration.

(FINERTY enters waving a newspaper.)

FINERTY. Savages! Savages killed Custer! The greatest general of our time, ambushed by savages! They *destroyed* the 7th Cavalry! Killed our next president...*(He exits.)*

BLACK ELK. The whites go insane. No treaty, no rule applies anymore. Wherever we go, they follow with overwhelming force. *(CRAZY HORSE begins to dance to the beat of the drum. A DRUMMER begins to sing— "The Trapped Dance.")*

DRUMMER.
Ampa luta wic zuya mani yo
Ampa luta wic zuya mani yo
Ampa luta wic zuya mani yo
Ampa luta wic zuya mani yo

(FOUR CAVALRY SOLDIERS dance on. They are "riding" horse dance sticks. The deadly game is Hide and Seek. CRAZY HORSE moves this way and that. He tries each of the four directions, but is always stopped by the SOLDIERS, always forced in other directions. The pace of the dance steadily increases. As the SOLDIERS charge, their horses kick the red sticks until the great hoop is destroyed and its pieces lie haphazardly about. CRAZY HORSE tricks the SOLDIERS, hides from them, and they gallop away. CRAZY HORSE crawls from his hiding place, moves center and comes to an exhausted stop. Even though

the remains of the Lakota staff have been lost in the struggle, he has eluded the army and is still free. He looks at the shattered remains of the hoop, picks up one of the pieces and raises it to the sky. When he turns toward home, he is met by starving RELATIVES. In his exhaustion, he tries to flee from this responsibility and slowly staggers toward each of the four directions. But this time, instead of meeting soldiers, he meets his tattered, starving people. Each of the four turns grows slower and more painful. At last, he comes to a complete stop. On the other side of the stage, isolated in a pool of light, is GENERAL CROOK. CRAZY HORSE stands for a moment staring at the STARVING LAKOTAS; he makes his decision and walks through them to the GENERAL.)

CROOK. Is it Crazy Horse?

CRAZY HORSE. I am responsible for many people. These people depend on me. Tell me what I can do so The People can have food.

CROOK. I've already suggested to my superiors that you be offered a reservation on the Powder River. *(CRAZY HORSE spins away from CROOK and struggles until he can control his emotions. He has promised himself that he will never lead his people to a reservation.)* Could your people live by the Powder?

CRAZY HORSE *(a long pause)*. Yes. We will move to the Powder.

CROOK *(hesitates)*. It's not entirely up to me. You must take your people to Fort Robinson and negotiate with the soldier chief.

CRAZY HORSE *(considers CROOK for a moment)*. I never wanted to fight. Except against the Crows, which is traditional. *(He again lifts the piece of broken hoop to the sky.)*

I will bring The People to Fort Robinson. *(The DRUM-MERS begin to sing— "The Long March"; the EAGLE SPIRIT begins to circle on the highest level. CRAZY HORSE exits; The STARVING LAKOTAS stagger to their feet and follow.)*

MUSICIANS.

> *Tehiya Mani pelo Hey ye ye ye ye*
> *Tehiya Mani pelo Hey ye ye ye ye*
> *Tehiya Mani pelo Hey ye ye ye ye*
> *Mita Kuye kin Mani pelo Hey ye—*

SCENE 5B
Fort Robinson, Nebraska, September 5, 1877

(FOUR STARVING LAKOTAS remove blankets and a buffalo robe to reveal FOUR SOLDIERS. They pick up pieces of the broken hoop, the remains of the Lakota staff and other abandoned possessions of the Lakotas, and push them into the junk-pile. The buffalo robe is placed DL with the hair side up. CRAZY HORSE appears on top of the ridge. He is followed by the STARVING LAKOTAS. They move down the ridge in a procession not unlike the Navajo walk to the Bosque Redondo. When CRAZY HORSE comes down from the ridge and crosses to the SERGEANT, the other SOLDIERS block the STARVING LAKOTAS from following.)

CRAZY HORSE *(looks at THE SOLDIERS, trying to perceive what is happening).* I come for peace. Now let The People eat. *(There is no answer.)* I come at the request of General Crook.

SERGEANT *(speaks with a faint German accent)*. General Crook has no jurisdiction at Fort Robinson.

CRAZY HORSE *(considers this)*. I come to negotiate with the soldier chief.

SERGEANT. The "soldier chief" is not available at this time. Perhaps tomorrow.

CRAZY HORSE *(testing)*. Yes. I will come back tomorrow. *(SOLDIERS surround CRAZY HORSE.)*

SERGEANT. You will stay here tonight. We have a place for you.

CRAZY HORSE *(a final effort)*. I prefer to spend the night out here on the grass with The People, under the sky.

SERGEANT. We have orders. This way, please.

CRAZY HORSE *(shoved forward)*. No. *(Controlled fury.)* I came under agreement to negotiate! I will not stay in a guard house! *(He is again pushed from behind.)* Do not touch me! I am Crazy Horse! *(TWO SOLDIERS try to wrench away the piece of the hoop CRAZY HORSE carries, but he will not let go. As the SOLDIERS lift the piece, CRAZY HORSE is stretched upward and the other SOLDIER rams a bayonet into his back. No sound comes from CRAZY HORSE; the scream of the mortally wounded comes from the STARVING LAKOTAS. The piece of hoop falls to the floor. CRAZY HORSE stands for a startled moment and then collapses in a writhing heap. The flute begins to wail. The EAGLE SPIRIT begins to flutter erratically. TWO SOLDIERS drag CRAZY HORSE to the buffalo robe and then join the other SOLDIERS to keep the STARVING LAKOTAS from moving to CRAZY HORSE. HOKSILA moves center to stare at the dying man.)*

BLACK ELK *(quietly to HOKSILA)*. All he ever wanted was to help The People; he fought only when the soldiers came to kill us. In battle, they could never defeat him; but they could lie to him and trick him in this way.

CRAZY HORSE *(with a great effort)*. Father, I want to see you! Mother, come to me!

FATHER'S VOICE. We cannot come.

MOTHER'S VOICE. They will not let us come!

CRAZY HORSE *(his voice weakening)*. Father, Mother...I want to see you.

BLACK ELK. We wait all night. Hundreds, in the dark, in a great circle, around the soldier doctor's hut. Then, at the far edge of the circle, some of the old women sense the moment.

CRAZY HORSE. Tell The People...tell them...they cannot depend on me any more. *(CRAZY HORSE struggles; then is dead. The flute falls silent. The EAGLE SPIRIT extends the wings, sends four piercing cries and then exits. The SOLDIERS exit. The FATHER OF CRAZY HORSE moves to the body, shouts three times to the sky. The DRUM-MERS sing—the "Crazy Horse Death Song.")*

MUSICIANS.

> *Oyate Ki Gowita Hey au ca*
> *Owi oki pi ca Ices mics zuyapo*
> *wicas Itancaki Ki Hena*
> *Mahpiyata Eya ye.*

(The MOTHER OF CRAZY HORSE and TWO WOMEN wrap the body in the buffalo robe and tie it with leather thongs. After the body of CRAZY HORSE is prepared, a WARRIOR places the remains of the Lakota staff on the wrapped body. He is joined by THREE other LAKOTA WARRIORS who lift the body to their shoulders and carry it off stage. The PARENTS and a LAKOTA WOMAN fol-low. The faces of the PARENTS and the WARRIORS are impassive. HOKSILA is openly weeping. The remaining

LAKOTAS recover the last pieces of the broken hoop and carry them off in various directions.)

BLACK ELK. The last great Lakota was buried in a private place near here. It does not matter where. *(The death song is finished. Silence. BLACK ELK speaks directly to HOKSILA.)* All that lasts is the earth. Like you, I, too, thought the white people must have some secret. I thought if I could see their world, I might discover the power of their secret and bring our hoop together again. Then, there came to us some men who wanted a few Oglalas to dance for a wild west show, Buffalo Bill's show, that would go across the great water to a big town, London.

SCENE 6
London, England, Spring, 1887

(From the place where Crazy Horse's funeral procession exited, the PARADE into the arena of a wild west show pours onto the stage. FOUR OGLALAS, carrying huge poster BANNERS, lead the procession. The MUSICIANS pound out a flashy version of Indian music— "Tenting To-night." This music, derived as much from the circus as from Lakota tradition, is played on a combination of native and wasichu "band" instruments. DANCERS, in gaudy show costumes, execute a frenetic fancy-dance. The images are blatantly and commercially exploitative. The WOMEN's shimmy is borrowed from burlesque houses rather than their culture. The MEN execute cliché war whoops as they chop the air with tomahawks. The specta-cle is seedy and painful.)

BLACK ELK. We danced for many people in that place. Then Grandmother England, Victoria, came in a big shining wagon to see us. Her dress was all shining, and her hat was all shining and so were the horses.

(A well-padded RELATIVE enters wearing a sparkling wasichu "formal" and a "crown.")

BLACK ELK. She looked like a fire coming.

QUEEN VICTORIA *(speaks in a broad, high British accent).* I am sixty-seven years old. All over the world I have seen all kinds of people, but today I have seen the best-looking people I know.

BLACK ELK. She was little and fat and we liked her.

QUEEN VICTORIA. If you belonged to me, I would not let them take you around and exhibit you like this. *(The poster BANNERS collapse; two of the RELATIVES spin wind-whistles and the sounds swirl across the stage; the "CAST," embarrassed and ashamed, disappears; the lights isolate BLACK ELK and HOKSILA. The sound of the wind-whistles merges with, and then is overtaken by, the sound of real wind that we heard in the opening scene.)*

SCENE 7
A Ceremonial Ground in the Black Hills, October, 1931

BLACK ELK. I discovered no secret; only that people would take everything from each other if they could; that people had forgotten that the earth is their mother. I became like a man who never had a vision. I was more and more sick to go home. I felt dead, my people lost, I thought I might never find them again. But Buffalo Bill had a strong heart and he came to help me. He gave me a ticket to go home, ninety dollars and medicine to help me sleep—to help me stop the dreams. *(Rumbles of thunder, filled with distant LAKOTA VOICES, cut through the wind.)* But, the medicine did not stop the Thunder Beings calling. Calling, "It is time! Hurry! The grandfathers are waiting!" *(The VOICES in the thunder call louder and more urgently. When THE OLD MAN replies, his voice is full of panic.)* How can I fulfill my mission when you never tell me what to do? *(The VOICES in the thunder call yet louder and more insistently. THE OLD MAN can stand the pressure no longer. Fifty years of frustration and anger erupt and he screams back to them.)* How can I hurry? I do not know what the Grandfathers expect. I do not know what you want me to do! *(Thunder roars back; BLACK ELK collapses; HOKSILA quickly reaches out, catches his grandfather and steadies him.)*

HOKSILA. Grandfather! It is enough. You must rest now.

BLACK ELK *(struggles to control his emotions)*. No. It is not finished. *(Desperate to complete his story, he compulsively resumes his narrative.)* When I reach home, I find our people, pitiful—in despair—living in square, gray houses on hungry land...and around them the white men have drawn a line to keep them in. Our only hope is in some strange news from the west. A Paiute holy man tells us a long time ago the Great Spirit sent his son to white people and they nailed him to a tree where he died. But now he is coming back, this time as an Indian, with light like a rainbow spreading around him; and he will come to us and there will be a new earth where only our people will live.

(A singer begins to sing—the "Ghost Dance Song." The RELATIVES, dressed in their drab reservation wear, enter

in single file and circle BLACK ELK and HOKSILA. Each
RELATIVE has untied his/her hair.)

BLACK ELK. The Holy Man promises that in the next
springtime, with the new grass appearing, another world is
coming—coming like a cloud, coming like a whirlwind out
of the west. All we have to do is dance; dance the dance of
the Ghosts and it will bring back our dead. *(As the drum*
moves into the heartbeat rhythm of the Ghost Dance, a
DRUMMER begins to sing as the RELATIVES clasp hands
and begin the dance.) All our people who ever lived will
be alive again, and all the buffalo, and all the other ani-
mals. Once more we will all be alive and together if we
dance the dance of the Ghosts. *(Seeking visions, each REL-*
ATIVE moves into his/her own ecstasy.) We hold hands
like the Santee on the gallows in Minnesota, touching one
another to say "I am here! I am here!" Big Foot's band of
Minneconjous begin to dance—widows, broken families,
they keep dancing till they faint because they want so
much to bring back those that have been killed. But the
government will not even let us dance! There is outrage
everywhere! The government agent at Pine Ridge tele-
graphs Washington, "Indians are dancing in the snow. We
need protection." Protection against dancing! Forces are as-
sembling, serious forces to stop our dancing, military
forces! We cannot contain any more brutality! We escape
into our visions...*(Now BLACK ELK begins to dance fe-*
verishly in the center of the circle. HOKSILA is frantic
with concern that the old man will not survive, but BLACK
ELK finds his vision, and his arms rise to the sky.)...we
see our beautiful land...green grass...fat horses...singing
hunters. We are in a great sacred circle...the hoop of our
Indian nation...and at the center is the sacred tree...and the

tree is in bloom! (*His hands drop. The RELATIVES in the circle continue to dance propelled by the vision of the new world to come, but it is no longer possible for BLACK ELK. All the suppressed emotion hidden through five hundred years of abuse releases—first anger, then great sorrow, then the joy of anticipation born of hope. Through it all, the dance continues.*) But, our dance is to be stopped. (*The dance freezes on the word "stopped."*) Soldiers are sent to arrest us.

Wounded Knee Creek, South Dakota, December 29, 1890

(*The winds howl as A RELATIVE twirls a wind-whistle. The other RELATIVES move through the bitter cold into six separate "camps."*)

BLACK ELK. Chief Big Foot has pneumonia; he lies in a wagon at Wounded Knee. Indian families huddle beside the frozen stream, Wounded Knee Creek. When the cavalry gallops up, Big Foot shows a white flag. Before dark the soldiers post Hotchkiss guns, cannons, on top of the rise overlooking this miserable camp. The soldiers belong to the 7th Cavalry once led by Custer. (*Wind-whistles out. BLACK ELK speaks quickly, clinically.*) At dawn they start taking away the weapons of these sick, freezing people— knives, a few rifles! A young deaf mute resists the order to give up his rifle. When they try to snatch the rifle away, it goes off, and they destroy us. (*The sound of drums mixes with that of cannons and rifles as the LAKOTAS are massacred. In the long silence after, we see the entire cast except BLACK ELK and HOKSILA sprawled about the stage in the grotesque frozen positions of violent death. Several bodies are entwined in the junk-pile.*) The winds have

reached us; they are blowing themselves out, blowing the
snow over us, one long grave for three hundred Indian people, people who had never done any harm, were only trying to run away, most of them women and children. For
this action; twenty six soldiers are awarded the Medal of
Honor. I did not know then how much was ending. When I
look back now from this high hill of my old age, I can still
see the butchered women and children and babies lying
heaped and scattered all along the crooked gulch as plain
as when I saw them with eyes still young. And I can see
that something else died there. I want you to see what else
died in the bloody snow and was buried in the blizzard. It
was a people's dream, a beautiful dream as you must
know, because it was your dream, too. *(He prays.)* O, Six
Grandfathers, hear me in my sorrow, for I may never call
again. The nation's hoop is broken and scattered. There is
no center any longer, and the sacred tree is dead. Today I
send a voice for people in despair. Hear me, not for myself, but for The People. O, make my people live.

HOKSILA. Grandfather, those winters are gone. *(The BOY
reaches under one of the bodies and pulls out a small piece
of a curved red stick; it is broken at one end and charred
at the other.)* The spring comes back with new grasses
showing tender faces to each other. So should we—the
two-leggeds with the four-leggeds, and the wings of the air
and all green things...together. *(HOKSILA carries the broken piece of the hoop D and places it where it used to be—
one tiny piece of what had been the huge hoop. A LITTLE
GIRL rises from the pile of bodies and walks toward the
broken stick and sits at one end of it.)*

BLACK ELK. Can it be that some small root of the sacred
tree still lives? A root that could be nourished? *(The sky
answers with a crash of thunder. The RELATIVES rise, one*

by one, and join the girl to complete the great circle. *BLACK ELK is unaware of them; he can see only the stick and the child. As the circle is completed, another clap of thunder splits the air and a magnificent rainbow arches across the sky. The size and intensity of the rainbow pushes HOKSILA to his knees, but it draws BLACK ELK upstage toward it until he stands by the ledge where he set the wooden cup at the beginning of the play. He picks up the cup, struggling to understand the meaning of these images that first appeared in his vision so many years ago.)* The voice said, "Behold this day, for it is yours to make. We offer the wooden cup filled with water. It is the power to make live. And it is yours." *(He turns to see his kneeling grandson untying his hair in the center of the circle. And then he comprehends.)* It is yours. *(Trembling with excitement, he carries the cup to HOKSILA. HOKSILA receives it, asks blessing from the sky and carries the cup downstage. Reaching across the piece of the broken hoop, he offers the cup to the audience.)*

HOKSILA. And it is yours...*(He moves to the audience on the right.)* and it is yours...*(He moves to the audience on the left.)* and it is yours. *(He turns back to where his grandfather is waiting in the center of the hoop.)*

    Meta Tunkasila ye yelo.

(The lights isolate BLACK ELK and HOKSILA.)

BLACK ELK. We have spoken.

BLACKOUT—END OF PLAY

DIRECTOR'S NOTES

DIRECTOR'S NOTES

DIRECTOR'S NOTES

DIRECTOR'S NOTES